The GREAT DIVIDE

Current and *Classic Quips*
on the *Battle* of the *Sexes*

STEPHEN WICKS

CB
CONTEMPORARY BOOKS

Library of Congress Cataloging-in-Publication Data
The great divide : current and classic quips on the battle of the
sexes / [collected by] Stephen Wicks.
     p.   cm.
    Includes bibliographic references and index.
    ISBN 0-8092-9951-8
      1. Man-woman relationships—Quotations, maxims,
etc.. I. Wicks, Stephen.
PN6084.M25G74   2000
305.3—dc21   00-34551
                                  CIP

Interior design by Monica Baziuk

Published by Contemporary Books
A division of NTC/Contemporary Publishing Group, Inc.
4255 West Touhy Avenue, Lincolnwood (Chicago), Illinois 60712-1975 U.S.A.
Printed in the United States of America
International Standard Book Number: 0-8092-9951-8
01 02 03 04 05 06 LB 17 16 15 14 13 12 11 10 9 8 7 6 5 4 3 2 1

Contents

INTRODUCTION   V

1. ACROSS THE GENDER GAP   I
   Men, Women, and the Battle of the Sexes

2. ALL ABOUT EVE   31
   Women—Feminism and Women's Roles—Beauty
   and Fashion—Motherhood

3. MALE CALL   77
   Men—Bachelors—Fatherhood—Boys

4. DATING AND RELATIONSHIPS   105
   Finding Someone So You Don't
   Have to Date Again

5. CUPID'S ARROW   119
   Love and Romance

6. SEX   133
   The Most Fun You Can Have Without Laughing

7. TAKING THE PLUNGE   167
   Marriage—Husbands—Wives—
   Weddings—Fidelity

8. MUCH "I DO" ABOUT NOTHING   201
   Divorce, Alimony, and Remarriage

BIBLIOGRAPHY   213

INDEX   225

Introduction

"In America," observed Marlene Dietrich, "sex is an obsession. In other parts of the world it is a fact."

An obsession indeed. And it seems that the turning of the millennium has done little to narrow the yawning gender gap.

Of course, the division of humankind into two sexes has infused our experience with intrigue and tension since, well, Adam and Eve. Few other subjects have prompted so many on both sides to question, reflect, or simply sound off. In the perpetual attempt to unravel the riddle of the sexes, men and women alike—novelists, playwrights, scholars, media figures, poets, philosophers, politicians, and humorists—have captured the mysteries and absurdities of sex with exceptional vividness from every imaginable perspective.

Between the pages of *The Great Divide* are more than one thousand of the funniest, most fascinating, and original things ever said about men, women, and their often complicated relationships. These quotations span history and represent diverse points of view from men and women of various backgrounds, professions, and cultures—suggesting that sex difference is as much a part of human experience as life and death.

It seems obvious from this collection that the 'great divide' between men and women never really narrows; it only changes its shape. As Henry Kissinger remarked, "No one will ever win the battle of the sexes. There's too much fraternizing with the enemy."

I agree. In fact, I think the battle of the sexes is one we willingly wage. As frustrating and confusing as the opposite sex can be, few people hold out long before going back for more.

This collection is a tribute to, and a celebration of, men, women, and everything that's right and wrong with all of us.

I could go on about men, women, and the Great Divide, but there's really no need. As you'll see when you turn the page, it's all been said before.

1

ACROSS THE GENDER GAP

Men, Women, and the Battle of the Sexes

When God created two sexes, He may
have been overdoing it.

—VARIOUSLY ATTRIBUTED

There is more difference within the sexes than between them.

—IVY COMPTON-BURNETT,
English writer

Women love cats. Men say they love cats, but when women aren't looking, men kick cats.

—MATT GROENING

In our civilization, men are afraid that they will not be men enough and women are afraid that they might be considered only women.

—THEODOR REIK,
Austrian psychologist

There is very little difference between men and women in space.

—HELEN SHARMAN,
Astronaut

Traditionally, men used power to gain sex, and women used sex to gain power.

—THOMAS SZASZ,
American psychiatrist

Men never remember, but women never forget.

—ANONYMOUS

The test of a man is how well he is able to feel about what he thinks. The test of a woman is how well she is able to think about what she feels.

—MARY McDOWELL,
Political activist

Men are superior to women. For one thing, they can urinate from a speeding car.

—WILL DURST,
American comedian

When a man gets up to speak, people listen, then look. When a woman gets up, people look; then, if they like what they see, they listen.

—PAULINE FREDERICK,
American journalist

Men are gentle, honest, and straightforward. Women are convoluted, deceptive, and dangerous.

—ERIN PIZZEY,
Writer and feminist critic

The vanity of men, a constant insult to women, is also the ground for the implicit feminine claim of superior sensitivity and morality.

> —PATRICIA MEYER SPACKS,
> *American scholar and writer*

Men mourn for what they've lost; women for what they ain't got.

> —JOSH BILLINGS,
> *American humorist*

Men act and women appear. Men look at women. Women watch themselves being looked at.

> —JOHN BERGER,
> *English art historian*

It is a known fact that men are practical, hard-headed realists. In contrast to women, who are romantic dreamers and actually believe that estrogenic skin cream must do something or they couldn't charge sixteen dollars for that tiny little jar.

> —JANE GOODSELL,
> *American writer*

Want him to be more of a man? Try being more of a woman!

—COTY PERFUME AD

It's too simple to say men and women are equal. You can't make equals of an apple and a pear; they're different.

—DUSTIN HOFFMAN

Men don't understand anything about women and women don't understand anything about men. And it's better that way.

—VITTORIO GASSMAN,
Italian actor

In the sex war, thoughtlessness is the weapon of the male, vindictiveness of the female.

—CYRIL CONNOLLY,
English journalist and editor

Ever since Eve gave Adam the apple, there has been a misunderstanding between the sexes about gifts.

—NAN ROBERTSON,
American journalist

The two sexes mutually corrupt and improve each
other.

—MARY WOLLSTONECRAFT SHELLEY

It is now possible for a flight attendant to get a pilot
pregnant.

—RICHARD J. FERRIS,
Former president, United Airlines

Mothers are fonder than fathers of their children
because they are more certain they are their own.

—ARISTOTLE

Until Eve arrived, this was a man's world.

—RICHARD ARMOUR,
American poet

What is most beautiful in virile men is something
feminine; what is most beautiful in feminine women
is something masculine.

—SUSAN SONTAG

When men reach their sixties and retire, they go to pieces. Women go right on cooking.

—GAIL SHEEHY

Whether women are better than men I cannot say—but I can say they are certainly no worse.

—GOLDA MEIR,
Israeli prime minister from 1969 to 1974

To be happy with a man, you must understand him a lot and love him a little. To be happy with a woman you must love her a lot and not try to understand her at all.

—HELEN ROWLAND,
English-American writer

All women become like their mothers. That is their tragedy. No man does. That's his.

—OSCAR WILDE

All women dress like their mothers. That is their tragedy. No man ever does. That's his.

—ALAN BENNETT,
English playwright

You see an awful lot of smart guys with dumb women, but you hardly ever see a smart woman with a dumb guy.

—ERICA JONG

More and more it appears that, biologically, men are designed for short, brutal lives and women for long, miserable ones.

—ESTELLE RAMEY, M.D.,
Georgetown School of Medicine

Women are always saying you never put the toilet seat back down. *Au contraire!* Women never put the seat back up. Women, who are always right, argue that a toilet seat belongs in the down position. Who says? The hinge works both ways. Whether you're sitting or standing, it's all a matter of perspective.

—JOEY O'CONNOR,
Author of Women Are Always Right
and Men Are Never Wrong

Men have a much better time of it than women. For one thing, they marry later; for another thing, they die earlier.

—H. L. MENCKEN,
American editor and satirist

If a man and woman, entering a room together, close the door behind them, the man will come out sadder and the woman wiser.

—H. L. MENCKEN,
American editor and satirist

Even the wisest men make fools of themselves about women, and even the most foolish women are wise about men.

—THEODOR REIK,
Austrian psychologist

Men live by forgetting, women live on memories.

—T. S. ELIOT

The only time a woman really succeeds in changing a man is when he's a baby.

—NATALIE WOOD

Woman wants monogamy; man delights in novelty.

—DOROTHY PARKER,
American writer, critic, and humorist

Women, as they grow older, rely more and more on cosmetics. Men, as they grow older, rely more and more on a sense of humor.

—GEORGE JEAN NATHAN,
American editor, writer, and critic

Hysteria is a natural phenomenon, the common denominator of the female nature. It's the big female weapon, and the test of a man is his ability to cope with it.

—TENNESSEE WILLIAMS

I suppose true sexual equality will come when a general called Anthea is found having an unwise lunch with a young, unreliable male model from Spain.

—JOHN MORTIMER,
English writer

Women are not men's equals in anything but responsibility. We are not their inferiors, either, or even their superiors. We are quite simply different races.

—PHYLLIS McGINLEY,
American writer

When man and woman die, as poets sung
His heart's the last part moves, her last, the tongue.

> —BENJAMIN FRANKLIN

Men and women are kneaded from the same dough.

> —RUSSIAN PROVERB

Men make houses, women make homes.

> —ANONYMOUS

The relations between men and women are like those
between Europe and the Indies: at once commerce
and a war.

> —NICOLAS CHAMFORT,
> *18th-century French writer and moralist*

The trouble in the world is nearly all due to the fact
that one half the people are men, and the other half,
women.

> —EDGAR WATSON HOWE,
> *19th-century American writer and editor*

A tranquil woman can go on sewing longer than an angry man can go on fuming.

—George Bernard Shaw

Of the two lots, the woman's lot of perpetual motherhood, and the man's of perpetual babyhood, I prefer the man's.

—George Bernard Shaw

None of us can boast much about the morality of our ancestors: the records do not show that Adam and Eve were married.

—Edgar Watson Howe,
19th-century American writer and editor

I love the idea of there being two sexes, don't you?

—James Thurber,
American writer and humorist

Women tend to qualify more than men. They put "perhaps" and "I think" and use diminutives more than men.

—Gail Godwin,
American writer

The gender gap is still there but no longer yawns as an all but unleapable chasm . . . Editors of national magazines no longer reply that they loved your poem, but they published a woman last month.

> —MAXINE KUMIN,
> *American poet*

The main difference between men and women is that men are lunatics and women are idiots.

> —REBECCA WEST,
> *English writer and critic*

Boy meets girl, so what?

> —BERTOLT BRECHT,
> *German playwright*

Women complain about sex more often than men. Their gripes fall into two major categories: 1) Not enough, 2) Too much.

> —ANN LANDERS

Women in love are less ashamed than men. They have less to be ashamed of.

> —AMBROSE BIERCE,
> *19th-century American journalist*

As vivacity is the gift of women, gravity is that of men.

> —JOSEPH ADDISON,
> *17th-century English writer and statesman*

The finest people marry the two sexes in their own person.

> —RALPH WALDO EMERSON

A male gynecologist is like an auto mechanic who doesn't own a car.

> —CARRIE SNOW,
> *Comedian*

A woman's head is always influenced by heart; but a man's heart by his head.

> —LADY MARGUERITE GARDINER BLESSINGTON,
> *19th-century English writer*

A man has to be Joe McCarthy to be called ruthless. All a woman has to do is put you on hold.

> —MARLO THOMAS

The great truth is that women actually like men, and men can never believe it.

> —ISABEL PATTERSON,
> *American writer*

Where young boys plan for what they will achieve and attain, young girls plan for whom they will achieve and attain.

> —CHARLOTTE PERKINS GILMAN,
> *American feminist and writer*

A man is as good as he has to be, and a woman as bad as she dares.

> —ELBERT HUBBARD,
> *American writer*

A man says what he knows, a woman says what will please.

> —JEAN-JACQUES ROUSSEAU,
> *18th-century French philosopher*

On one issue men and women agree: they both distrust women.

> —H. L. MENCKEN,
> *American editor and satirist*

There are three sexes—men, women, and clergymen.

—SYDNEY SMITH,
19th-century English writer and clergyman

Three sexes in America—men, women, and
professors.

—JOEL E. SPINGARN,
American civil rights activist

A man is a person who will pay two dollars for a one-
dollar item he wants. A woman will pay one dollar for
a two-dollar item she doesn't want.

—WILLIAM BINGER

Men and women should live next door and visit each
other once in a while.

—KATHARINE HEPBURN

Men and women are two locked caskets, of which
each contains the key to the other.

—ISAK DINESEN,
Danish writer

Woman reaches love through friendship; man reaches friendship through love.

> —MUHAMMAD HIJAZI,
> *Persian writer*

Equal rights for the sexes will be achieved when mediocre women occupy high positions.

> —FRANCOISE GIROUD,
> *French writer and former minister of culture*

Men and women are like right and left hands: it doesn't make sense not to use both.

> —JEANNETTE RANKIN,
> *American suffragist*

Man without woman would be as stupid a game as playing checkers alone.

> —JOSH BILLINGS,
> *American humorist*

Conversation between Adam and Eve must have been difficult at times because they had nobody to talk about.

> —AGNES REPPLIER,
> *American essayist*

The man's desire is for the woman; the woman's desire is for the desire of man.

> —SAMUEL TAYLOR COLERIDGE,
> *English poet, critic, and essayist*

The first kiss is stolen by the man; the last is begged by the woman.

> —H. L. MENCKEN,
> *American editor and satirist*

I refuse to believe that trading recipes is silly. Tuna-fish casserole is as least as important as corporate stock.

> —BARBARA GRIZZUTI HARRISON,
> *American writer*

A good cigar is as great a comfort to a man as a good cry is to a woman.

> —EDWARD BULWER-LYTTON,
> *19th-century English writer*

Temptation is a woman's weapon and a man's excuse.

> —H. L. MENCKEN

Toughness doesn't have to come in a pinstripe suit.

> —DIANNE FEINSTEIN,
> *American politician*

I think older women with younger men threaten all the right people.

> —WILLIAM HAMILTON,
> *American editorial cartoonist, in 1996*

When men meet a bride, they look at her face, but women look at her clothes.

> —EDGAR WATSON HOWE,
> *19th-century American writer and editor*

Freud is the father of psychoanalysis. It has no mother.

> —GERMAINE GREER,
> *English writer*

Women are programmed to love completely, and men are programmed to spread it around.

> —BERYL BAINBRIDGE,
> *English writer*

Adam could not be happy even in Paradise
without Eve.

> —JOHN LUBBOCK,
> *19th-century English naturalist,*
> *banker, and statesman*

It is rare that one can see in a little boy the promise of
a man, but one can almost always see in a little girl the
threat of a woman.

> —ALEXANDRE DUMAS,
> *19th-century French writer and playwright*

Adultery is a stimulant to men, but a sedative to
women.

> —MALCOLM DE CHAZAL,
> *Surrealist writer*

I wish I could change my sex as I change my shirt.

> —ANDRÉ BRETON,
> *French writer*

Men are brought up to command, women to seduce.

> —SALLY KEMPTON,
> *American writer and feminist*

Instead of this absurd division into sexes, they ought to class people as static or dynamic.

—EVELYN WAUGH

Men seem to kick friendship around like a football, but it doesn't seem to crack. Women treat it as glass and it goes to pieces.

—ANNE MORROW LINDBERGH,
American writer and poet

A man is designed to walk three miles in the rain to phone for help when the car breaks down—and a woman is designed to say, "You took your time" when he comes back dripping wet.

—VICTORIA WOOD,
English writer, comedian, and singer

When men and women agree it is only in their conclusions; their reasons are always different.

—GEORGE SANTAYANA,
American philosopher

Boys will be boys these days, and so, apparently will girls.

—Jane Howard,
American journalist

If American men are obsessed with money, American women are obsessed with weight. The men talk of gain, the women talk of loss, and I do not know which talk is the more boring.

—Marya Mannes,
American journalist

What men and women need is encouragement. . . . Instead of always harping on a man's faults, tell him of his virtues. Try to pull him out of his rut of bad habits.

—Eleanor H. Porter,
19th-century American writer

A lady is smarter than a gentleman, maybe. She can sew a fine seam, she can have a baby, she can use her intuition instead of her brain. But she can't fold a paper in a crowded train.

—Phyllis McGinley,
American writer

A man's brain has a more difficult time shifting from thinking to feeling than a woman's brain does.

> —BARBARA DE ANGELIS,
> *American psychologist*

And when a woman's will is as strong as the man's who wants to govern her, half her strength must be concealment.

> —GEORGE ELIOT

And yet wherever there exists the display of power there is politics, and in women's relations with men there is a continual transfer of power, [so] there is, continually, politics.

> —SALLY KEMPTON,
> *American writer and feminist*

Except for their genitals, I don't know what immutable differences exist between men and women. Until social expectations . . . are equal, until we provide equal respect for both sexes, answers to this question will simply reflect our prejudices.

> —NAOMI WEISSTEIN,
> *American psychologist and activist*

Men are just as vain as women, and sometimes even more so.

—HELENA RUBINSTEIN,
Business executive and philanthropist

I came to live in a country I love; some people label me a defector. I have loved men and women in my life; I've been labeled "the bisexual defector." Want to know another secret? I'm even ambidextrous. I don't like labels. Just call me Martina.

—MARTINA NAVRATILOVA

I do not believe in sex distinction in literature, law, politics, or trade—or that modesty and virtue are more becoming to women than to men, but wish we had more of it everywhere.

—BELVA LOCKWOOD,
19th-century American social reformer and lawyer

I earn and pay my own way as a great many women do today. Why should unmarried women be discriminated against—unmarried men are not.

—DINAH SHORE

I tell you there isn't a thing under the sun that needs to be done at all, but what a man can do better than a woman, unless it's bearing children, and they do that in a poor make-shift way; it had better have been left to the men.

—GEORGE ELIOT

Instead of getting hard ourselves and trying to compete, women should try to give their best qualities to men—bring them softness, teach them how to cry.

—JOAN BAEZ

It is strange that modesty is the rule for women when what they most value in men is boldness.

—NINON DE LENCLOS,
17th-century French courtesan

Men and women belong to different species, and communication between them is a science still in its infancy.

—BILL COSBY

Nature is just enough; but men and women must comprehend and accept her suggestions.

—ANTOINETTE BROWN BLACKWELL,
19th-century American abolitionist and feminist

Our duty, as men and women, is to proceed as if limits to our ability did not exist. We are collaborators in creation.

—PIERRE TEILHARD DE CHARDIN,
French philosopher and paleontologist

People don't have fortunes left them in that style nowadays; men have to work and women to marry for money. It's a dreadfully unjust world.

—LOUISA MAY ALCOTT

The first problem for all of us, men and women, is not to learn, but to unlearn.

—GLORIA STEINEM

The sexes in each species of being . . . are always true equivalents—equals but not identical.

—ANTOINETTE BROWN BLACKWELL

The woman's vision is deep reaching, the man's far reaching. With the man the world is his heart, with the woman the heart is her world.

—BETTY GRABLE

To be womanly is one thing, and one only; it is to be sensitive to man, to be highly endowed with the sex instinct; to be manly is to be sensitive to woman.

—JANE HARRISON,
English scholar, writer, and archeologist

We women ought to put first things first. Why should we mind if men have their faces on the money, as long as we get our hands on it?

—IVY BAKER PRIEST,
American government official

Women have invented nothing . . . except male babies who grew up to be men big enough to be killed fighting.

—JANET FLANNER,
American journalist

Theories by women about women have only recently begun to appear in print. Theories by men about women are abundant.

—PATRICIA MEYER SPACKS,
American columnist and writer

What women want is what men want. They want respect.

—MARILYN VOS SAVANT,
American columnist and writer

I think we're here for each other.

—CAROL BURNETT

Beauty is the wisdom of women. Wisdom is the beauty of men.

—CHINESE PROVERB

Most women have all other women as adversaries;
most men have all other men as their allies.

> —GELETT BURGESS,
>   *American humorist*

If it's true that men are such beasts, this must account
for the fact that most women are animal lovers.

> —DORIS DAY

2

ALL ABOUT EVE

Women—Feminism and Women's Roles—
Beauty and Fashion—Motherhood

Being a woman is of special interest only
to aspiring male transsexuals. To actual
women, it is merely a good excuse
not to play football.

—FRAN LEBOWITZ

Women

The female sex has no greater fan than I, and I have the bills to prove it.

> —ALAN J. LERNER,
> *American playwright and composer*

The great question which has never been answered and which I have not yet been able to answer, despite my 30 years of research into the feminine soul is: What do women want?

> —SIGMUND FREUD

One should never trust a woman who tells one her real age. A woman who would tell one that, would tell one anything.

> —OSCAR WILDE

I must have women. There is nothing unbends the mind like them.

> —JOHN GAY,
> *18th-century English poet and playwright*

Women over thirty are at their best, but men over thirty are too old to recognize it.

—JEAN-PAUL BELMONDO,
French actor

There are always women who will take men on their own terms. If I were a man I wouldn't bother to change while there are women like that around.

—ANN OAKLEY,
American writer

Too many women don't realize they're women and that disturbs me.

—LEE MARVIN

In most action movies, women are in the way.

—ARNOLD SCHWARZENEGGER

Directing is more fun with women—everything is.

—INGMAR BERGMAN

The way to a woman's heart is through your wallet.

—ANONYMOUS

A kiss can be a comma, a question mark, or an exclamation point. That's basic spelling that every woman ought to know.

—MISTINGUETT,
French dancer and singer

What do I look for in women? Clean knickers.

—JAMES CAAN

Women are more difficult to handle than men. It's their minds.

—PETER SELLARS

Why is it OK for men to go around topless when some of them have bigger boobs than many women?

—JILL CLAYBURGH

You have the kind of breasts I could take home to my mother.

—ANONYMOUS FAN,
to Susan Sarandon

For *Star Wars*, they had me tape down my breasts because there are no breasts in space. I have some. I have two.

—CARRIE FISHER

Intimacies between women often go backwards, beginning in revelations and ending up in small talk without loss of esteem.

—ELIZABETH BOWEN,
Irish-American writer

If Miss means respectably unmarried, and Mrs. means respectably married, then Ms. means nudge, nudge, wink, wink.

—ANGELA CARTER,
English writer

Women are most fascinating between the ages of thirty-five and forty, after they have won a few races and know how to pace themselves. Since few women ever pass forty, maximum fascination can continue indefinitely.

—CHRISTIAN DIOR

What else goes wrong for a woman, except her marriage?

—Euripides

Have you noticed how many books are written about women in the course of one year? Have you any notion how many are written by men? Are you aware that you are, perhaps, the most discussed animal in the universe?

—Virginia Woolf

Women request estimates from contractors before remodeling their houses, and they wouldn't hire a new employee without a reference check, yet they easily fall into bed with a new man without knowing a thing about his character, his track record, or his intentions.

—Helena Hacker Rosenberg,
American writer

My eleven-year-old daughter mopes around the house all day waiting for her breasts to grow.

—Bill Cosby

The lovely thing about being forty is that you can appreciate twenty-five-year-old men more.

> —COLLEEN MCCULLOUGH,
> *Australian writer*

For a single woman, preparing for company means wiping the lipstick off the milk carton.

> —ELAYNE BOOSLER,
> *Comedian*

I shrug my shoulders in despair at women who moan at the lack of opportunities and then take two weeks off as a result of a falling out with their boyfriends.

> —SOPHIE MIRMAN,
> *Entrepreneur and businesswoman*

Women are always eagerly on the lookout for any emotion.

> —STENDHAL,
> *19th-century French writer*

Do you not know I am a woman? When I think, I must speak.

> —WILLIAM SHAKESPEARE

It was a woman who drove me to drink and you know, I never even thanked her.

—W. C. FIELDS

Women prefer poverty with love to luxury without it.

—THE TALMUD

Women do not find it difficult nowadays to behave like men, but they often find it difficult to behave like gentlemen.

—COMPTON MACKENZIE,
English writer

A total woman caters to her man's special interests, whether it be salads, sex, or sports.

—MARABEL MORGAN,
Author of The Total Woman

I heard a man say that brigands demand your money or your life, whereas women require both.

—SAMUEL BUTLER,
19th-century English writer

On one issue, at least, men and women agree: they both distrust women.

    —H. L. MENCKEN,
      American editor and satirist

The way to fight a woman is with your hat. Grab it and run.

    —JOHN BARRYMORE

A woman will flirt with anybody in the world as long as other people are looking on.

    —OSCAR WILDE

How much fame, money, and power does a woman have to achieve on her own before you can punch her in the face?

    —P. J. O'ROURKE,
      American journalist and humorist

A witch and a bitch always dress up for each other, because otherwise the witch would upstage the bitch, or the bitch would upstage the witch, and the result would be havoc.

    —TENNESSEE WILLIAMS

It would be practically impossible to write an accurate novel about the quality of life for single women in New York without writing a B novel, for the simple reason that life for single women in New York is a B novel.

—Nora Ephron,
American writer

There comes a time in every woman's life when the only thing that helps is a glass of champagne.

—Bette Davis,
in Old Acquaintance*, 1943*

Friendship among women is only a suspension of hostilities.

—Antoine De Rivarol,
18th-century French journalist

Never try to impress a woman, because if you do she'll expect you to keep up to the standard for the rest of your life.

—W. C. Fields

Women give us solace, but if it were not for women
we should never need solace.

>—Don Herold,
>*American writer and humorist*

What passes for woman's intuition is often nothing
more than man's transparency.

>—George Jean Nathan,
>*American editor, writer, and critic*

The prostitute is the only honest woman left in
America.

>—Ti-Grace Atkinson,
>*American feminist*

No woman has ever stepped on Little America—and
we have found it to be the most silent and peaceful
place in the world.

>—Richard E. Byrd,
>*Polar explorer*

If you can make a woman laugh you can do anything
with her.

>—Nicol Williamson,
>*Scottish actor*

Woman is at once Apple and Serpent.

—HEINRICH HEINE,
19th-century German poet

Educating a woman is like pouring honey into a fine
Swiss watch: everything stops.

—KURT VONNEGUT

A woman is always buying something.

—OVID,
Roman poet

A woman is only a woman, but a good cigar is a
smoke!

—RUDYARD KIPLING

A species that cannot love an automobile.

—BERNARD DEVOTO,
American historian and critic

Women have two weapons—cosmetics and tears.

—NAPOLEON BONAPARTE

A bad woman raises hell with a good many men,
while a good woman raises hell with only one.

> —EDGAR WATSON HOWE,
>   *19th-century American writer and editor*

No woman is all sweetness; even the rose has thorns.

> —MME. RÉCAMIER,
>   *18th-century French society figure*

There is no female mind. The brain is not an organ of
sex. Might as well speak of a female liver.

> —CHARLOTTE PERKINS GILMAN,
>   *American feminist and writer*

The cleverest woman finds a need for foolish
admirers.

> —ANONYMOUS

You will find that the woman who is really kind to
dogs is always one who has failed to inspire sympathy
in men.

> —MAX BEERBOHM,
>   *English writer and critic*

One of the few lessons I have learned in life is that
there is invariably something odd about women who
wear ankle socks.

> —ALAN BENNETT,
> *English playwright and actor*

Good women always think that it is their fault when
someone else is being offensive. Bad women never
take the blame for anything.

> —ANITA BROOKNER,
> *English writer*

Women would rather be right than be reasonable.

> —OGDEN NASH,
> *American poet*

The great and almost only comfort about being a
woman is that one can always pretend to be more
stupid than one is and no one is surprised.

> —DAME FREYA STARK,
> *English explorer and writer*

A lady is one who never shows her underwear
unintentionally.

—LILLIAN DAY,
Writer

Some women are like Pompeii; some are like Verdun;
some are like Kokomo, Indiana, on a Sunday
afternoon.

—BENJAMIN DE CASSERES,
American writer

Man has his will—but woman has her way!

—OLIVER WENDELL HOLMES, SR.

A lady is nothing very specific: one man's lady is
another man's woman; sometimes, one man's lady is
another man's wife.

—RUSSELL LYNES,
American editor and writer

In the theater, a hero is one who believes that all
women are ladies; a villain, one who believes all ladies
are women.

—GEORGE JEAN NATHAN,
American editor, writer, and critic

Women are repeatedly accused of taking things personally. I cannot see any other honest way of taking them.

> —MARYA MANNES,
> *American journalist*

I'm not denyin' the women are foolish: God almighty made 'em to match the men.

> —GEORGE ELIOT

All women are misfits, I think: we do not fit into this world without amputations.

> —MARGE PIERCY,
> *American writer*

Women never have young minds. They are born three thousand years old.

> —SHELAGH DELANEY,
> *English writer*

In my youth there were words you couldn't say in front of a girl; now you can't say *girl*.

> —TOM LEHRER,
> *American entertainer*

All women are lesbians, except those who don't know it yet.

> —JILL JOHNSTON,
> *Writer and feminist*

A woman is like a teabag. Only in hot water do you realize how strong she is.

> —NANCY REAGAN

Every woman is a science.

> —JOHN DONNE,
> *English poet*

The female of the species is more deadly than the male.

> —RUDYARD KIPLING

Wicked women bother one. Good women bore one. That is the only difference between them.

> —OSCAR WILDE

When I was very young, I kissed my first woman, and smoked my first cigarette on the same day. Believe me, never since have I wasted any more time on tobacco.

> —ARTURO TOSCANINI,
> *Italian conductor*

Women are not much, but they are the best other sex we have.

> —DON HEROLD,
> *American writer and humorist*

Women should be obscene and not heard.

> —JOHN LENNON

There are only two kinds of women—goddesses and doormats.

> —PABLO PICASSO

Once a woman has given her heart you can never get rid of the rest of her.

> —JOHN VANBRUGH,
> *English playwright and architect*

Only good girls keep diaries. Bad girls don't have the time.

—Tallulah Bankhead

An intelligent woman is a woman with whom one can be as stupid as one wants.

—Paul Valery,
French poet and critic

Women are most adorable when they are afraid; that's why they frighten so easily.

—Ludwig Boerne,
German writer

If a woman likes another woman, she's cordial. If she doesn't like her, she's very cordial.

—Irvin S. Cobb,
American humorist and journalist

Nine times out of ten, a woman had better show more affection than she feels.

—Jane Austen

Women who love the same man have a kind of bitter freemasonry.

—MAX BEERBOHM,
English writer and critic

The fear of women is the basis of good health.

—SPANISH PROVERB

When a woman tells you her age, it's alright to look surprised, but don't scowl.

—WILSON MIZNER,
American playwright

Show me a woman who doesn't feel guilty and I'll show you a man.

—ERICA JONG

A lady's imagination is very rapid; it jumps from admiration to love, from love to matrimony in a moment.

—JANE AUSTEN

When women go wrong, men go right after them.

—MAE WEST

These impossible women! How they do get
   around us!
The poet was right: can't live with them, or
   without them!

   —ARISTOPHENES

There are girls who manage to sell themselves, whom
no one would take as gifts.

   —NICOLAS CHAMFORT,
   18th-century French writer and moralist

If she is pleasing to one man, a girl is taken care of.

   —PROPERTIUS,
   Roman poet

There's nothing like mixing with woman to bring out
all the foolishness in a man of sense.

   —THORNTON WILDER

A pessimist is a man who thinks all women are bad.
An optimist is one who hopes they are.

   —CHAUNCEY M. DEPEW,
   American attorney and politician

Personally, I think if a woman hasn't met the right man by the time she's 24, she may be lucky.

> —JEAN KERR,
> *Writer and humorist*

I am a woman meant for a man, but I never found a man who could compete.

> —BETTE DAVIS,
> *Attributed*

A woman without a man cannot meet a man, any man . . . without thinking, even if it's for a half-second, perhaps this is *the* man.

> —DORIS LESSING,
> *English writer and playwright*

Aren't women prudes if they don't and prostitutes if they do?

> —KATE MILLETT,
> *American feminist*

The modern rule is that every woman must be her own chaperone.

> —AMY VANDERBILT,
> *American etiquette authority*

A woman never sees what we do for her, she only sees what we don't do.

—GEORGES COURTELINE,
19th-century French humorist

We love women in proportion to their degree of strangeness to us.

—CHARLES BAUDELAIRE,
19th-century French poet

When I say I know women, I mean that I know that I don't know them.

—WILLIAM THACKERAY,
19th-century English writer

Being a woman is a terribly difficult task, since it consists principally in dealing with men.

—JOSEPH CONRAD

To be a woman is something so strange, so confusing, and so complicated that only a woman could put up with it.

—KIERKEGAARD,
Danish philosopher

Women are the sex which believes that if you charge it, it's not spending; and if you add a cherry to it, it's not intoxicating.

—BILL VAUGHAN,
American journalist

He gets on best with women who know how to get on without them.

—AMBROSE BIERCE,
19th-century American journalist

The hardest problem of a girl's life is to find out why a man seems bored if she doesn't respond to him, and frightened if she does.

—HELEN ROWLAND,
English-American writer

Is there a way to accept the concept of the female orgasm and still command the respect of your foreign auto-mechanic?

—BRUCE FEIRSTEIN,
Writer

One tongue is sufficient for a woman.

—JOHN MILTON,
17th-century English poet

Nothing is more intolerable than a wealthy woman.

—JUVENAL,
Roman satirist

I will not say that women have no character; rather they have a new one every day.

—HEINRICH HEINE,
19th-century German poet

Women sometimes forgive those who force an opportunity, never those who miss it.

—TALLEYRAND,
18th-century French diplomat

Between a woman's "yes" and "no" I would not venture to stick a pin.

—MIGUEL DE CERVANTES SAAVEDRA,
16th-century Spanish writer

There are few virtuous women who are not weary of their profession.

—LA ROCHEFOUCAULD,
17th-century French moralist

She is chaste whom nobody has asked.

—OVID,
Roman poet

Feminism and Women's Roles

Women who insist upon having the same options as men would do well to consider the option of being the strong, silent type.

—FRAN LEBOWITZ

A liberated woman is one who has sex before marriage and a job after.

—GLORIA STEINEM

Misogynist: a man who hates women as much as women hate one another.

—H. L. MENCKEN,
American editor and satirist

Don't you realize that as long as you have to sit down
to pee, you'll never be a dominant force in the world?
You'll never be a convincing technocrat or middle
manager. Because people will know. She's in there
sitting down.

> —Don DeLillo,
> *American writer*

I myself have never been able to find out precisely
what feminism is: I only know that people call me a
feminist whenever I express sentiments that
differentiate me from a doormat.

> —Rebecca West,
> *English writer and critic*

No man is as anti-feminist as a really feminine
woman.

> —Frank O'Connor,
> *Irish writer and critic*

People are just not very ambitious for women still.
Your son you want to be the best he can be. Your
daughter you want to be happy.

> —Alexa Canady,
> *First African-American female neurosurgeon*

Nature has given women so much power that the law
has very wisely given them little.

—SAMUEL JOHNSON,
18th-century English writer

A woman who *thinks* she's intelligent demands
equal rights with men. A woman who *is* intelligent
does not.

—COLETTE,
French writer

They have a right to work wherever they want to—as
long as they have dinner ready when you get home.

—JOHN WAYNE

It is a pity that so often the only way to treat girls like
people seems to be to treat them like boys.

—KATHERINE WHITEHORN,
English writer

We are becoming the men we wanted to marry.

—GLORIA STEINEM

Surely that shove I feel between my shoulder blades
isn't liberation?

—JILL TWEEDIE,
English writer and feminist

A caress is better than a career.

—ELIZABETH MARBURY,
American playwright, in 1933

I never realized until lately that women were
supposed to be the inferior sex.

—KATHARINE HEPBURN

You've come a long way, baby.

—VIRGINIA SLIMS CIGARETTES AD SLOGAN

We haven't come a long way, we've come a short way.
If we hadn't come a short way, no one would be
calling us "baby."

—ELIZABETH JANEWAY,
American writer

I would say that the majority of women (happily for society) are not much troubled with sexual feeling of any kind.

> —DR. WILLIAM ACTON,
> *English physician, in 1857*

There are three intolerable things in life—cold coffee, lukewarm champagne, and over-excited women.

> —ORSON WELLES

The only trouble with sexually liberating women is that there aren't enough sexually liberated men to go around.

> —GLORIA STEINEM

Women have gone through a real revolution in this country. They have started trusting one another.

> —MARLO THOMAS

Woman is the nigger of the world.

> —YOKO ONO

The claim that American women are downtrodden
and unfairly treated is the fraud of the century.

—PHYLLIS SCHLAFLY,
Conservative political activist

Your concern for the rights of women is especially
    welcome news.
I'm sure you'd never exploit one;
I expect you'd rather be dead;
I'm thoroughly convinced of it—
Now can we go to bed?

—WENDY COPE,
English poet

Being a lady war correspondent is like being a lady
wrestler—You can be one of them at a time, but not
both simultaneously.

—DICKEY CHAPELLE,
*American journalist, killed covering the Vietnam
War in 1965*

When a woman becomes a scholar there is usually
something wrong with her sex organs.

—FRIEDRICH NIETZSCHE

Women must pay for everything . . . They do get more glory than men for comparable feats. But, also, women get more notoriety when they crash.

—AMELIA EARHART

Being a woman has only bothered me in climbing trees.

—FRANCES PERKINS,
First female U.S. cabinet member

Of my two "handicaps," being female always put many more obstacles in my path than being black.

—SHIRLEY CHISHOLM,
First African-American woman elected to Congress

Married women are kept women, and they are beginning to find out.

—LOGAN PEARSALL SMITH,
English writer and critic

I must not write a word to you about politics because you are a woman.

—JOHN ADAMS,
in a letter to Abigail Adams

Women's studies is a jumble of vulgarians, bunglers, whiners, French faddicts, apparatchiks, doughface party-liners, pie-in-the-sky-utopianists, and bullying, sanctimonious sermonizers.

—CAMILLE PAGLIA

The only options open for girls then were of course mother, secretary, or teacher. At least that's what we all thought and were preparing ourselves for. Now I must say how lucky we are, as women, to live in an age where "dental hygenist" has been added to the list.

—ROSEANNE

It used to be almost the first question (just after "Can you type?") in the standard female job interview: "Are you now, or have you ever, contemplated marriage, motherhood, or the violent overthrow of the U.S. government?"

—BARBARA EHRENREICH,
American writer

Once I tried to explain to a fellow feminist why I liked wearing make-up: she replied by explaining why she does not. Neither of us understood a word the other said.

—Nora Ephron,
American writer

The major concrete achievement of the women's movement in the 1970s was the Dutch treat.

—Nora Ephron

A woman without a man is like a fish without a bicycle.

—Gloria Steinem,
Attributed

Social progress can be measured exactly by the social position of the fair sex—the ugly ones included.

—Karl Marx

Whatever women do they must do twice as well as men to be thought half as good. Luckily, this is not difficult.

—Charlotte Whitton,
Former mayor of Ottawa

The vote, I thought, means nothing to women. We should be armed.

—EDNA O'BRIEN,
  Irish writer and pacifist

Fat Is a Feminist Issue

—TITLE OF BOOK BY SUSIE ORBACH

Well-behaved women rarely make history.

—LAUREL THATCHER ULRICH,
  American historian

Beauty and Fashion

She got her good looks from her father. He's a plastic surgeon.

—GROUCHO MARX

A ship is always referred to as "she" because it costs so much to keep one in paint and powder.

—CHESTER NIMITZ,
  American admiral

You'd be surprised how much it costs to look this cheap.

—DOLLY PARTON

I don't mind being naked because I like the sensuality of a nice body. Trouble is, food is fun and exercise is boring.

—BO DEREK

I can't bear being seen nearly naked. I'm not exactly a tiny woman. When Sophia Loren is naked, this is a lot of nakedness.

—SOPHIA LOREN

A dress makes no sense unless it inspires men to want to take it off you.

—FRANÇOISE SAGAN,
French writer

Just because a dress is red satin does not mean it will come off easily.

—ANONYMOUS

Your dresses should be tight enough to show that
you're a woman and loose enough to show you're a
lady.

> —EDITH HEAD,
> *American costume designer*

It was a blond. A blond to make a bishop kick a hole
in a stained-glass window.

> —RAYMOND CHANDLER,
> *in* Farewell, My Lovely, *1940*

"Where should one wear perfume?" a young woman
asked. "Wherever one wants to be kissed," I said.

> —COCO CHANEL

Everything you see I owe to spaghetti.

> —SOPHIA LOREN

Where do you go to get anorexia?

> —SHELLEY WINTERS

If I have only one life, let me live it as a blond!

> —CLAIROL AD SLOGAN

Plain women know more about men than beautiful ones do.

—KATHARINE HEPBURN

There are no ugly women. Only lazy ones.

— HELENA RUBINSTEIN,
Business executive and philanthropist

I gave my beauty and my youth to men. I am going to give my wisdom and experience to animals.

—BRIGITTE BARDOT

Behind every successful man you'll find a woman— who has absolutely nothing to wear.

—JAMES STEWART

There is no cosmetic for beauty like happiness.

—LADY MARGUERITE GARDINER BLESSINGTON,
19th-century English writer

She that paints her Face, thinks of her Tail.

—BENJAMIN FRANKLIN

Beauty is the first present nature gives to women and the first it takes away.

—Variously attributed

A girl whose cheeks are covered with paint, has an advantage with me over one whose ain't.

—Ogden Nash,
American poet

Even the most respectable woman has a complete set of clothes in her wardrobe ready for a possible abduction.

—Sacha Guitry,
French actor and playwright

A beautiful woman should break her mirror early.

—Baltasar Gracian,
17th-century Spanish writer and priest

Any girl can be glamorous. All you have to do is stand still and look stupid.

—Hedy Lamarr

As a ring of a gold in a swine's snout, so is a beautiful woman who lacks discretion.

—THE BIBLE,
Proverbs 11:22

A whore in a fine dress is like a dirty house with a clean door.

—SCOTTISH PROVERB

I'm not ugly, but my beauty is a total creation.

—TYRA BANKS

These days, putting out one's pretty power, one's pussy power, one's sexual energy for popular consumption no longer makes you a bimbo—it makes you smart. So now, all of a sudden, actresses and models whose livelihoods aren't in trouble take it all off for *Playboy* . . . The nude photographs are a career move, and it says: I've got it, and goddamn it I'm going to flaunt it because anyone can think I'm a bimbo, but not just anyone can look this good naked.

—ELIZABETH WURTZEL,
Author of Bitch

I never expected to see the day when girls would get sunburned in the places they do now.

> —WILL ROGERS,
> *Attributed*

Clothes are our weapons, our challenges, our visible insults.

> —ANGELA CARTER,
> *English writer*

Where women are concerned, the rule is never to go out with anyone better dressed than you.

> —JOHN MALKOVICH

When a woman isn't beautiful, people always say, "You have lovely eyes, you have lovely hair."

> —ANTON CHEKHOV

I always say beauty is only sin deep.

> —SAKI,
> *Scottish writer*

If beauty is truth, why don't women go to the library to have their hair done?

—Lily Tomlin

The body of a young woman is God's greatest achievement . . . Of course, he could have built it to last longer but you can't have everything.

—Neil Simon

When I began, at least women dressed to please men. Now, they dress to astonish one another.

—Coco Chanel

Put the light out, and all women are alike.

—German proverb

Handsome women generally fall to the lot of ugly men.

—Italian proverb

All heiresses are beautiful.

—John Dryden,
17th-century English poet

The best thing is to look natural, but it takes makeup
to look natural.

—CALVIN KLEIN

A woman is as young as her knee.

—MARY QUANT,
English fashion designer

Motherhood

My biological clock is ticking so loudly I'm nearly
deafened by it. They search me going into planes.

—MARIAN KEYES,
Irish writer

I like trying to get pregnant. I'm not so sure about
childbirth.

—LAUREN HOLLY,
American actress

Having a baby is like taking your lower lip and
forcing it over your head.

—CAROL BURNETT

I didn't know how babies were made until I was
pregnant with my fourth child.

—LORETTA LYNN

A pregnant woman wants toasted snow.

—HEBREW PROVERB

It is not the glass ceiling that holds women back from
rising high, it is the children hanging on to their
hems.

—POLLY TOYNBEE,
English columnist

Often women have babies because they can't think of
anything better to do.

—LORD BEAUMONT OF WHITLEY,
16th-century English playwright

Somewhere on this globe, every ten seconds, there is
a woman giving birth to a child. She must be found
and stopped.

—SAM LEVENSON,
American comic

Only when a woman decides not to have children,
can a woman live like a man. That's what I've done.

    —KATHARINE HEPBURN

Our bodies are shaped to bear children, and our lives
are a working out of the processes of creation. All our
ambitions and intelligence are beside that great
elemental point.

    —PHYLLIS MCGINLEY,
     American writer

Women who emasculate are called "mothers."

    —ABIGAIL VAN BUREN

The hand that rocks the cradle rules the world.

    —PROVERB

The hand that rules the cradle rocks the world.

    —PETER DEVRIES,
     American writer and humorist

A fluent tongue is the only thing a mother doesn't like her daughter to resemble in her.

> —RICHARD BRINSLEY SHERIDAN,
> *18th-century English-Irish playwright*

Being the mother of a teenager is a strange and precarious experience. You both know about sex, but nobody's talking. Better to talk about cannibalism.

> —CYNTHIA HEIMEL,
> *American writer*

If pregnancy were a book they would cut the last two chapters.

> —NORA EPHRON,
> *American writer*

No matter how old a mother is she watches her middle-aged children for signs of improvement.

> —FLORIDA SCOTT-MAXWELL,
> *American writer*

3

MALE CALL

Men—Bachelors—Fatherhood—Boys

Years ago, manhood was an opportunity
for achievement, and now it is a problem
to be overcome.

—GARRISON KEILLOR

Men

The way to a man's heart is through his stomach.

> —Fanny Fern,
>   *19th-century columnist*
>   *and writer*

Anybody who believes that the way to a man's heart is through his stomach flunked geography.

> —Robert Byrne,
>   *American writer and editor*

Any smart woman will tell you that the best way to a man's heart is through his ego.

> —Anonymous

The one thing that men and women have in common—they both like the company of men.

> —Michael Douglas

I don't see many men today. I see a lot of guys running around television with small waists, but I don't see many men.

> —Anthony Quinn

I've always liked men better than women.

—BETTE DAVIS

I don't mind living in a man's world as long as I can be a woman in it.

—MARILYN MONROE

It is a man's world, and you men can have it.

—KATHERINE ANNE PORTER,
American writer

My ancestors wandered lost in the wilderness for 40 years because even in biblical times, men would not stop to ask for directions.

—ELAYNE BOOSLER,
Comedian

Men build bridges and throw railways across deserts, and yet they contend successfully that the job of sewing on a button is beyond them. Accordingly, they don't have to sew buttons.

—HEYWOOD C. BROUN,
American journalist

A man who has no office to go to . . . I don't care
who he is . . . is a trial of which you can have no
conception.

> —GEORGE BERNARD SHAW

Success has made failures of many men.

> —CINDY ADAMS,
> *Celebrity columnist*

If you're looking for a man who's attractive, funny,
smart, self-confident, sensitive, sexy, affectionate, and
romantic, go to the movies.

> —BRUCE LANSKY,
> *American writer and editor*

I don't believe man is a woman's natural enemy.
Perhaps his lawyer is.

> —SHANA ALEXANDER,
> *American news commentator*

Tell me why it is that every man who seems attractive
these days is either married or barred on a
technicality.

> —CELESTE HOLM

To women, we are like big dogs that talk.

—LARRY MILLER,
Comedian

The bravest thing that men do is love women.

—MORT SAHL

I took up a collection for a man in our office. But I didn't get enough money to buy one.

—RUTH BUZZI

I refuse to consign the whole male sex to the nursery. I insist on believing that some men are my equals.

—BRIGID BROPHY,
English-Irish writer

Great men are not always idiots.

—KAREN ELIZABETH GORDON,
American writer

Can you imagine a world without men? No crime and lots of happy fat women.

—MARION SMITH,
Comedian

I don't know why women want any of the things men have when one of the things women have is men.

—COCO CHANEL

I'm a simple man. All I want is enough sleep for two normal men, enough whiskey for three, and enough women for four.

—JOEL ROSENBERG,
Science fiction writer

If men knew all that women think, they'd be twenty times more daring.

—ALPHONSE KARR,
19th-century French writer

A man who has never made a woman angry is a failure in life.

—CHRISTOPHER MORLEY,
American journalist

That common cold of the male psyche, fear of commitment.

—RICHARD SCHICKEL,
Film critic

It takes a woman twenty years to make a man of her
son, and another woman twenty minutes to make a
fool of him.

—HELEN ROWLAND,
  English-American writer

Men adore women. Our mothers taught us to.
Women do not adore men; women are amused by
men, we are a source of chuckles.

—GARRISON KEILLOR

I think we're a kind of desperation. We're sort of a
maddening luxury. The basic and essential human
being is the woman, and all that we're doing is trying
to brighten up the place. That's why all the birds who
belong to our sex have prettier feathers, because males
have got to try and justify their existence.

—ORSON WELLES

To really know a man, observe his behavior with a
woman, a flat tire, and a child.

—ANONYMOUS

They came out with a new perfume that's bound to be a sure hit with men. It smells like beer.

—SUSAN SAVANNAH,
American humor writer

OK, so maybe I am saying guys are scum. But they're not mean-spirited scum. And few of them—even when they are out of town on business trips and have a clear cut opportunity—will poop on the floor.

—DAVE BARRY

Some men are so macho they'll get you pregnant just to kill a rabbit.

—MAUREEN MURPHY,
Comedian

Women speak because they wish to speak, whereas a man speaks only when driven to speech by something outside himself, like, for instance, he can't find any clean socks.

—JEAN KERR,
American writer and humorist

Men know they are sexual exiles. They wander the earth seeking satisfaction, craving and despising, never content. There is nothing in that anguished motion for women to envy.

—CAMILLE PAGLIA

It's hard for men to find the best strategy for campaigning against a woman. It's like hitting a marshmallow. Either you appear too aggressive or as though you can't handle it.

—SENATOR NANCY KASSENBAUM,
in 1984

If men can run the world, why can't they stop wearing neckties? How intelligent is it to start the day by tying a little noose around your neck?

—LINDA ELLERBEE

Whatever they may be in public life, whatever their relations with men, in their relations with women, all men are rapists, and that's all they are. They rape us with their eyes, their laws, and their codes.

—MARILYN FRENCH,
Feminist writer

You're not too bright. I like that in a man.

—KATHLEEN TURNER,
in Body Heat, *1981*

A monogamous man is like a bear riding a bicycle: he can be trained to do it, but he would rather be in the woods doing what bears do.

—GARRISON KEILLOR

On why men won't ask directions:
If you're a guy driving a car, and you don't know how to get where you're going, and you pull over to ask another guy, and he *does* know, then he is legally entitled to *take your woman!*

—DAVE BARRY

Men should not care too much for good looks. Neglect is becoming.

—OVID,
Roman poet

A man in the house is worth two in the street.

—MAE WEST

History is bright and fiction dull with homely men who have charmed women.

—O. Henry

Probably the only place where a man can feel really secure is in a maximum security prison, except for the imminent threat of release.

—Germaine Greer,
  English reformer and writer

If they can put one man on the moon, why can't they put them all there?

—Variously attributed

No nice men are good at getting taxis.

—Katherine Whitehorn,
  English writer

What most men desire is a virgin who is a whore.

—Edward Dahlberg,
  American writer

The same time that women came up with PMS, men came up with ESPN.

    —Blake Clark,
     Actor and comedian

Beware of men who cry. It's true that men who cry are sensitive and in touch with feelings, but the only feelings they tend to be in touch with are their own.

    —Nora Ephron,
     American writer

I have yet to hear a man ask for advice on how to combine marriage and a career.

    —Gloria Steinem

I've never gone anywhere where the men have come up to my infantile expectations.

    —Rebecca West,
     English writer and critic

Men do not settle down. Men surrender.

    —Chris Rock

Men have been taught to deal only with what they
understand. This is what they respect. They know
that somewhere feeling and knowledge are important,
so they keep women around to do their feeling for
them, like ants do aphids.

> —AUDRE LORDE,
>   *American poet*

Macho does not prove mucho.

> —ZSA ZSA GABOR

There are two things no man will ever admit he
cannot do well: drive and make love.

> —STIRLING MOSS,
>   *English auto racer*

I love men, not because they are men, but because
they are not women.

> —CHRISTINA,
>   *Queen of Sweden from 1632 to 1654*

Y'know the problem with men? After the birth, we're
irrelevant.

> —DUSTIN HOFFMAN

Few men know how to kiss well; fortunately, I've always had time to teach them.

—MAE WEST

Any man who says he doesn't desire to have sex with a woman he thinks is attractive is lying.

—CORBIN BERNSEN

There's nothing so stubborn as a man when you want him to do something.

—JEAN GIRAUDOUX,
French writer and diplomat

A man is as old as the woman he feels.

—GROUCHO MARX

A man is so in the way in the house!

—ELIZABETH GASKELL,
19th-century English writer

Men are those creatures with two legs and eight hands.

—JAYNE MANSFIELD

Men are the enemy, but I still love the enemy.

> —RENEE ZELLWEGER,
> *in* Jerry Maguire, *1996*

Men always fall for frigid women because they put on the best show.

> —FANNY BRICE,
> *American singer and comedian*

If men could get pregnant, abortion would be a sacrament.

> —FLORYNCE KENNEDY,
> *American feminist and writer*

Men are always doomed to be duped . . . They are always wooing goddesses, and marrying mere mortals.

> —WASHINGTON IRVING,
> *19th-century American historian and writer*

The true man wants two things: danger and play. For that reason he wants woman as the most dangerous plaything.

> —FRIEDRICH NIETZSCHE

However much men say sex is not on their minds all the time, it is—most of the time.

—Jackie Collins

Most men who run down women are only running down a certain woman.

—Rémy de Gourmont,
  19th-century French critic

Men lose more conquests by their own awkwardness than by any virtue in the woman.

—Ninon de Lenclos,
  17th-century French courtesan

If a man doesn't look at me when I walk into a room, he's gay.

—Kathleen Turner

Italian men want to make sure you know they've got a penis.

—W. H. Auden

Many men have little use for small talk.

> —DEBORAH TANNEN,
> *American sociolinguist*

Nothing is so silly as the expression of a man who is being complimented.

> —ANDRÉ GIDE,
> *French writer and critic*

Energy is more attractive than beauty in a man.

> —LOUISA MAY ALCOTT

The game women play is men.

> —ADAM SMITH,
> *18th-century English economist and philosopher*

Male sexual response is far brisker and more automatic. It is triggered easily by things—like putting a quarter in a vending machine.

> —DR. ALEX COMFORT,
> *Author of* The Joy of Sex

I love men like some people like good food and wine.

—GERMAINE GREER,
English reformer and writer

A man running after a hat is not half so ridiculous as a man running after a woman.

—G. K. CHESTERTON,
English writer

A man would never get the notion of writing a book on the peculiar situation of the human male.

—SIMONE DE BEAUVOIR,
French writer

A man is given the choice between loving women and understanding them.

—NINON DE LENCLOS,
17th-century French courtesan

I only like two kinds of men: domestic and foreign.

—MAE WEST

If man knew how women pass the time when they are alone, they'd never marry.

—O. HENRY

Men are nicotine soaked, beer besmirched, whiskey greased, red-eyed devils.

—CARRY NATION,
American social reformer

Men are so willing to respect anything that bores them.

—MARILYN MONROE

Men cease to interest us when we find their limitations.

—RALPH WALDO EMERSON

She's just using him to keep from being by herself. That's the worst use of a man you can have.

—AUGUST WILSON,
American playwright

Some men are like nails, very easily drawn; others however are more like rivets never drawn at all.

—JOHN BURROUGHS,
19th-century American naturalist

The harder you try to hold onto them, the easier it is for some gal to pull them away.

—AUGUST WILSON,
American playwright

To a smart girl men are no problem—they're the answer.

—ZSA ZSA GABOR

When a man keeps beating me to the draw mentally, he begins to get glamorous.

—ZORA NEALE HURSTON,
American playwright and writer

I mean to make myself a man, and if I succeed in that,
I shall succeed in everything else.

—JAMES A. GARFIELD,
19th-century American president

I never liked the men I loved, and never loved the
men I liked.

—FANNY BRICE,
American singer and comedian

Most men lead lives of quiet desperation and go to the
grave with the song still in them.

—HENRY DAVID THOREAU

You can always spot a well-informed man—his views
are the same as yours.

—ILKA CHASE,
American actress and writer

Men are too emotional to vote. Their conduct
at baseball games and political conventions shows
this . . .

—ALICE DUER MILLER,
American writer

Men aren't the way they are because they want to
drive women crazy; they've been trained to be that
way for thousands of years. And that training makes it
very difficult for men to be intimate.

—BARBARA DE ANGELIS,
American psychologist

The success of any man with any woman is apt to
displease even his best friends.

—MADAME DE STAËL,
18th-century French writer

Guys are simple . . . women are not simple and they
always assume that men must be just as complicated as
they are, only way more mysterious. The whole point
is guys are not thinking much. They are just what
they appear to be. Tragically.

—DAVE BARRY

I know a lot of men who are healthier at age fifty than they have ever been before, because a lot of their fear is gone.

> —ROBERT BLY,
> *American poet*

Bachelors

A bachelor is a man who comes to work each morning from a different direction.

> —SHALOM ALEICHEM,
> *19th-century American humorist*

Show me a man who lives alone and has a perpetually clean kitchen, and 8 times out of 9, I'll show you a man with detestable spiritual qualities.

> —CHARLES BUKOWSKI,
> *American writer*

I've always held that a bachelor is a fellow who never makes the same mistake once.

> —GARY COOPER,
> *in* Northwest Mounted Police, *1940*

The only good husbands stay bachelors; they're too considerate to get married.

> —FINLEY PETER DUNNE,
> *American journalist and humorist*

The bachelor is a peacock, the engaged man a lion, the married man a jackass.

> —GERMAN PROVERB

I would be married, but I'd have no wife,
I would be married to a single life.

> —RICHARD CRASHAW,
> *17th-century English poet*

Certainly the best works, and of greatest merit for the public, have proceeded from the unmarried, or childless man.

> —FRANCIS BACON,
> *English philosopher and statesman*

A bachelor is a man who is right sometimes.

> —ANONYMOUS

Fatherhood

The fundamental defect of fathers is that they want their children to be a credit to them.

>—BERTRAND RUSSELL,
> *English philosopher and mathematician*

Paternity is a career imposed on you without any inquiry into your fitness.

>—ADLAI STEVENSON,
> *American politician*

Every father expects his boy to do the things he wouldn't do when he was young.

>—KIN HUBBARD,
> *American journalist and humorist*

Boys

Of all the animals, the boy is the most unmanageable.

>—PLATO

A boy is a hurry on its way to doing nothing.

>—JOHN CIARDI,
> *American poet*

The fact that boys are allowed to exist at all is evidence of a remarkable Christian forebearance among men.

—AMBROSE BIERCE,
19th-century American journalist

"When I get to be a man!" Being human, though boys, they considered their present estate too commonplace to be dwelt upon. So, when the old men gather, they say: "When I was a boy!" It really is the land of nowadays that we never discover.

—BOOTH TARKINGTON,
American writer and playwright

Boys are found everywhere on top of, underneath, inside of, climbing on, swinging from, running around or jumping to. Mothers love them, little girls hate them, older sisters and brothers tolerate them, adults ignore them and Heaven protects them.

—ALAN BECK,
in "What Is a Boy?," a pamphlet distributed by the
New England Life Insurance Company, 1956

I pay the schoolmaster, but 'tis the schoolboys that educate my son.

—RALPH WALDO EMERSON

Men get opinions as boys learn to spell, by reiteration chiefly.

—ELIZABETH BARRETT BROWNING

My object will be, if possible, to form Christian men, for Christian boys I can scarcely hope to make.

—THOMAS ARNOLD,
19th-century English educator

Only little boys and old men sneer at love.

—LOUIS AUCHINCLOSS,
American writer

There comes a time in every rightly constructed boy's life when he has a raging desire to go somewhere and dig for hidden treasure.

—MARK TWAIN

A man can never quite understand a boy, even when he has been a boy.

—G. K. CHESTERTON,
English writer

Boys will be boys—and so will a lot of middle-aged men.

> —KIN HUBBARD,
> *American journalist and humorist*

Boys are beyond the range of anybody's sure understanding, at least when they are between the ages of 18 months and 90 years.

> —JAMES THURBER,
> *American writer and humorist*

Boys do not grow up gradually. They move forward in spurts like the hands of clocks in railway stations.

> —CYRIL CONNOLLY,
> *English journalist and editor*

I am fond of children—except boys.

> —LEWIS CARROLL

4

DATING AND RELATIONSHIPS

Finding Someone
So You Don't Have to Date Again

It is possible for a woman to be happy
without a man, but not if she wants to be
rescued. If you're waiting to be rescued,
you never do anything but get your legs
waxed.

—CYNTHIA HIEMEL,
Writer and humorist

Never approach a friend's girlfriend with mischief as your goal. There are just too many women in the world to justify that sort of dishonorable behavior. Unless she's really attractive.

—BRUCE FRIEDMAN,
Writer

The chick in her thirties who still insists on meeting men in bars has told herself that she really wants the kind of guy you meet in bars, and she deserves what she gets.

—JULIE TILSNER,
Author of 29 and Counting: A Chick's Guide to Turning 30

There are times not to flirt. When you're sick. When you're with children. When you're on the witness stand.

—JOYCE JILLSON,
Astrologer

Because sex on the first date, or sooner if possible, is his goal, does not mean that the man feels he owes the woman anything. In fact, if she succumbs too quickly, she might lose her chance at the movie (unless the movie involves some kind of martial arts, since he was definitely going to see it anyway).

—MERRILL MARKOE,
  American writer

Flirting is the gentle art of making a man feel pleased with himself.

—HELEN ROWLAND,
  English-American writer

If you are living with a man, you don't have to worry about whether you should sleep with him after dinner.

—STEPHANIE BRUSH,
  Humor writer and columnist

With the catching end the pleasures of the chase.

—ABRAHAM LINCOLN

If you never want to see a man again, say: "I love you;
I want to marry you; I want to have children"—they
leave skid marks.

>—RITA RUDNER

Men seldom make passes
At girls who wear glasses.

>—DOROTHY PARKER,
>   *American writer, critic, and humorist*

Boys don't make passes at female smart-asses.

>—LETTY COTTIN POGREBIN,
>   *American writer*

The ultimate test of a relationship is to disagree but to
hold hands.

>—ALEXANDRA PENNEY,
>   *American writer*

When you're in a relationship, you're always
surrounded by a ring of circumstances . . . joined
together by a wedding ring, or in a boxing ring.

>—BOB SEGER

If you are looking for a kindly, well-to-do older gentleman who is no longer interested in sex, take out an ad in *The Wall Street Journal*.

—ABIGAIL VAN BUREN

Early to bed and early to rise, and your girl will go out with other guys.

—ANONYMOUS

A relationship is what happens between two people who are waiting for something better to come along.

—ANONYMOUS

My boyfriend and I broke up. He wanted to get married, and I didn't want him to.

—RITA RUDNER

Never date a woman you can hear ticking.

—MARK PATINKIN,
Columnist

Dating: Finding someone so you won't have to date again.

—SUSAN ST. JAMES

The perfect lover is one who turns into a pizza at
4:00 A.M.

—CHARLES PIERCE,
American female impersonator

Dating is always a problem for women. The man who
looks as if he may be a good husband, probably is.

—ANONYMOUS

If the right man does not come along, there are many
fates far worse. One is to have the wrong man come
along.

—LETITIA BALDRIDGE,
Etiquette columnist

I have such poor vision I can date anybody.

—GARRY SHANDLING

Look for a sweet person.
Forget rich.

—ESTEE LAUDER

Whenever I want a really nice meal, I start dating again.

—SUSAN HEALY,
Comedian

I can't get a relationship to last longer than it takes to make copies of their tapes.

—MARGARET SMITH,
Writer and comedian

The only useful thing about chemistry is that it explains why you always fall for jerks.

—BRUCE LANSKY,
American writer and editor

In more instances than I care to remember the men to whom I've been irresistibly attracted would have been more attracted to my brother.

—LINDA BIRD FRANCKE,
Editor, columnist, and writer

I'm always attracted to the wrong kind of guy—like the Pope.

—CAROL LEIFER,
Comedian

Her face was her chaperone.

—RUPERT HUGHES,
American writer, director, and screenwriter

The soundtrack to *Indecent Exposure* is a romantic mix of music that I know most women love to hear, so I never keep it far from me when women are nearby.

—FABIO

These men, it's not like we don't see them coming. Our intuition is good; the problem is we ignore it.

—AMY HEMPEL,
American writer

Do not discuss bondage on the first date.

—LINDA SUNSHINE,
American writer

I met this guy who said he loved children. Then I found out he was on parole for it.

—MONICA PIPER,
American writer

When someone asks, "Why do you think he's not calling me?" there's always one answer—"He's not interested." There's not ever any other answer.

—FRAN LEBOWITZ

A girl can wait for the right man to come along but in the meantime that still doesn't mean she can't have a wonderful time with all the wrong ones.

—CHER

How many of you have ever started dating because you were too lazy to commit suicide?

—JUDY TENUTA,
American comedian

From my experience of life I believe my own personal motto should be "Beware of men bearing flowers."

—MURIEL SPARK,
Scottish writer

When you live alone, you can be sure that the person who squeezed the toothpaste tube in the middle wasn't committing a hostile act.

—ELLEN GOODMAN,
Columnist

I think men talk to women so they can sleep with them and women sleep with men so they can talk to them.

—JAY MCINERNEY,
American writer

Maybe the most that you can expect from a relationship that goes bad is to come out of it with a few good songs.

—MARIANNE FAITHFULL,
Songwriter and musician

Don't grab a girl the moment you get into a taxicab. At least wait until the driver puts down the flag.

—GEORGE JEAN NATHAN,
American editor, writer, and critic

It's terrific if you're a computer.

—RITA MAE BROWN

I have noticed before that there is a category of acquaintanceship that is not friendship or business or romance, but speculation, fascination.

—JANE SMILEY

Intimate relationships cannot substitute for a life plan. But to have any meaning or viability at all, a life plan must include intimate relationships.

—HARRIET LERNER,
American therapist and writer

Never idealize others. They will never live up to your expectations. Don't over-analyze your relationships. Stop playing games. A growing relationship can only be nurtured by genuineness.

—LEO BUSCAGLIA,
American writer and educator

Oh, the comfort, the inexpressible comfort of feeling safe with a person, having neither to weigh thoughts nor measure words, but pouring them all right out, just as they are, chaff and grain together . . .

—DINAH MULOCK CRAIK,
19th-century English writer

Relationships are like a dance, with visible energy racing back and forth between partners. Some relationships are the slow, dark dance of death.

—COLETTE DOWLING,
  American writer

The cocktail party . . . is a device either for getting rid of social obligations hurriedly en masse or for making overtures toward more serious social relationships, as in the etiquette of whoring.

—BROOKS ATKINSON,
  American drama critic

There is a rule in sailing where the more maneuverable ship should give way to the less maneuverable craft. I think this is sometimes a good rule to follow in human relationships as well.

—DR. JOYCE BROTHERS

There is probably nothing like living together for blinding people to each other.

—IVY COMPTON-BURNETT,
  English writer

Underground issues from one relationship or context invariably fuel our fires in another.

—HARRIET LERNER,
American therapist and writer

My success has allowed me to strike out with a higher class of women.

—WOODY ALLEN

5

CUPID'S ARROW

Love and Romance

Love is the delightful interval between
meeting a beautiful girl and discovering
that she looks like a haddock.

—JOHN BARRYMORE

Love is a gross exaggeration of the difference between one person and everybody else.

—GEORGE BERNARD SHAW

Love does not consist in gazing at each other, but in looking out together in the same direction.

—ANTOINE DE SAINT-EXUPÉRY,
French writer and aviator

A proof that experience is of no use, is that the end of one love does not prevent us from beginning another.

—PAUL BOURGET,
19th-century French writer

If only one could tell true love from false love the way one can tell mushrooms from toadstools.

—KATHERINE MANSFIELD,
New Zealand writer

Let the first impulse pass, wait for the second.

—BALTASAR GRACIAN,
17th-century Spanish writer and priest

What then in love can woman do? If we grow fond
they shun us. And when we fly them, they pursue:
But leave us when they've won us.

—JOHN GAY,
18th-century English poet and playwright

One seeks to make the loved one entirely happy, or, if
that cannot be, entirely wretched.

—JEAN DE LA BRUYERE,
17th-century French poet and playwright

A guy knows he's in love when he loses interest in his
car for a couple of days.

—TIM ALLEN

In love, you pay as you leave.

—MARK TWAIN

Love is the only disease that makes you feel better.

—SAM SHEPARD,
American playwright and actor

Everything we do in life is based on fear, especially love.

—MEL BROOKS

One is very crazy when in love.

—SIGMUND FREUD

It's an extra dividend when you like the girl you're in love with.

—CLARK GABLE

Ah, love—the walks over soft grass, the smiles over candlelight, the arguments over just about everything else.

—MAX HEADROOM

True love comes quietly, without banners or flashing lights. If you hear bells, get your ears checked.

—ERICH SEGAL,
American writer

All's fair in love and war.

—PROVERB

If love is shelter, I'm going to walk in the rain.

—Anonymous

You can't buy love, but you can pay heavily for it.

—Henny Youngman,
American comedian

Love is the same as like except you feel sexier.

—Judith Viorst,
American writer

I've only been in love with a beer bottle and a mirror.

—Sid Vicious

Love matches are made by people who are content,
for a month of honey, to condemn themselves to a life
of vinegar.

—Lady Marguerite Gardiner Blessington,
19th-century English writer

Love is just a system for getting someone to call you
darling after sex.

—Julian Barnes,
English writer

No one has ever loved anyone the way everyone wants to be loved.

> —MIGNON McLAUGHLIN,
> *American journalist*

The most exciting attractions are between two opposites that never meet.

> —ANDY WARHOL

Love is a snowmobile racing across the tundra and then suddenly it flips over, pinning you underneath. At night, the ice weasels come.

> —MATT GROENING

In the spring a young man's fancy turns to thoughts
       of love;
And in summer,
and in autumn,
and in winter—
See above.

> —E. Y. HARBURG,
> *American lyricist*

Love is a game—yes?
I think it is a drowning.

> —AMY LOWELL,
> *American poet*

Is not general incivility the very essence of love?

> —JANE AUSTEN

He that is not jealous is not in love.

> —AUGUSTINE,
> *4th-century philosopher and religious figure*

Love is a fire. But whether it's going to warm your
hearth or burn down your house, you can never tell.

> —JOAN CRAWFORD

Love is being stupid together.

> —PAUL VALÉRY,
> *French poet and critic*

I love Mickey Mouse more than any woman I've ever
known.

> —WALT DISNEY

In love there are two things: bodies and words.

—Joyce Carol Oates

Friendship often ends in love; but love in friendship—never.

—Charles Caleb Colton,
  19th-century English writer

To be loved at first sight, a man should have at the same time something to respect and something to pity in his face.

—Stendhal,
  19th-century French writer

Love is what happens to a man and a woman who don't know each other.

—W. Somerset Maugham,
  English writer

Love as a relation between men and women was ruined by the desire to make sure of the legitimacy of children.

—Bertrand Russell,
  English philosopher and mathematician

Many a man has fallen in love with a woman in a light so dim he would not have chosen his suit by it.

—MAURICE CHEVALIER,
French actor and singer

Love is much nicer to be in than an automobile accident, a tight girdle, a higher tax bracket, or a holding pattern over Philadelphia.

—JUDITH VIORST,
American writer

Love is the strange bewilderment which overtakes one person on account of another person.

—JAMES THURBER AND E. B. WHITE

I'll believe [in love] when girls of twenty with money marry male paupers, turned sixty.

—ELBERT HUBBARD,
American writer

Love is an irresistible desire to be irresistibly desired.

—ROBERT FROST,
Attributed

Love will never be ideal until man recovers from the illusion that he can be just a little bit faithful or a little bit married.

—HELEN ROWLAND,
English-American writer

The lover thinks of possessing his mistress more often than her husband thinks of guarding his wife.

—STENDHAL,
19th-century French writer

If two people love each other there can be no happy end to it.

—ERNEST HEMINGWAY

Love is a kind of warfare.

—OVID,
Roman poet

Love is what you feel for a dog or a pussy cat. It doesn't apply to humans.

—JOHNNY ROTTEN,
English punk rocker

When people say, "You're breaking my heart," they do in fact usually mean that you're breaking their genitals.

> —JEFFREY BERNARD,
> *English columnist*

Love means not ever having to say you're sorry.

> —ERICH SEGAL,
> *American writer*

Love is the extremely difficult realization that something other than oneself is real.

> —IRIS MURDOCH,
> *Irish writer*

The prerequisite for making love is to like someone enormously.

> —HELEN GURLEY BROWN

If love is the answer, could you please rephrase the question?

> —LILY TOMLIN

Of course there is such a thing as love, or there wouldn't be so many divorces.

> —EDGAR WATSON HOWE,
> *19th-century American writer and editor*

Love is the effort a man makes to be satisfied with only one woman.

> —PAUL GERALDY,
> *French poet and playwright*

The moment I even say to a woman: I love you!—my love dies down considerably.

> —D. H. LAWRENCE

The course of true love never did run smooth.

> —WILLIAM SHAKESPEARE

I love her too, but our neuroses just don't match.

> —ARTHUR MILLER

This being in love is great—you get a lot of compliments and begin to think you are a great guy.

> —F. SCOTT FITZGERALD

In a great romance, each person basically plays a part that the other really likes.

—ELIZABETH ASHLEY,
American actress

Romance is the glamour which turns the dust of everyday life into a golden haze.

—ELINOR GLYN,
English writer

Romance like a ghost escapes touching; it is always where you are not, not where you are. The interview or conversation was prose at the time, but it is poetry in the memory.

—GEORGE WILLIAM CURTIS,
19th-century American writer and editor

We romantic writers are there to make people feel and not think. A historical romance is the only kind of book where chastity really counts.

—BARBARA CARTLAND,
English writer

6

SEX

The Most Fun You Can Have
Without Laughing

Who would have ever thought you
could die from sex? It was much more
fun when you only went to hell.

—JOHN WATERS,
American filmmaker

I can remember when the air was clean and sex was
dirty.

    —George Burns

It is not true that sex degrades women . . . if it is any
good.

    —Alan Partridge,
      of BBC radio

I hate a woman who offers herself because she ought
to do so, and, cold and dry, thinks of her sewing
when she's making love.

    —Ovid,
      Roman poet

Never play cards with any man named "Doc."
Never eat at any place called "Mom's."
And never, never, no matter what else you do in your
whole life, never sleep with anyone whose troubles
are worse than your own.

    —Nelson Algren,
      American writer

Girls who put out are tramps. Girls who don't are
ladies. This is, however, a rather archaic use of the
word. Should one of you boys happen upon a girl
who doesn't put out, do not jump to the conclusion
that you have found a lady. What you have probably
found is a lesbian.

—FRAN LEBOWITZ

There are a number of mechanical devices which
increase sexual arousal, particularly in women. Chief
among these is the Mercedes-Benz 380SL convertible.

—P. J. O'ROURKE,
American journalist and humorist

Genitals are a great distraction to scholarship.

—MALCOLM BRADBURY,
English writer

A kiss is an application for a better position.

—JEFF ROVIN,
American writer

What do you say if you really do have a headache?

—BRUCE LANSKY,
American writer and editor

It's OK to laugh in the bedroom as long as you don't point.

> —WILL DURST,
> *American comedian*

I have a self-esteem problem. During sex I fantasize that I'm someone else.

> —RICHARD LEWIS,
> *American comedian*

The only people who make love all the time are liars.

> —TELLY SAVALAS

For birth control I rely on my own personality.

> —MILT ABEL,
> *American comedian*

Condoms aren't completely safe. A friend of mine was wearing one and got hit by a bus.

> —BOB RUBIN,
> *American comedian and writer*

More divorces start in the bedroom than in any other room in the house.

—ANN LANDERS

An intellectual is someone who has found one thing that's more interesting than sex.

—ALDOUS HUXLEY,
English writer

I consider promiscuity immoral. Not because sex is evil, but because sex is too good and too important.

—AYN RAND

Sex is a three-letter word which needs some old-fashioned four-letter words to convey its full meaning.

—ANONYMOUS

Sex without love is merely healthy exercise.

—ROBERT HEINLEIN,
American writer

I had no idea so many people in the United States and Canada were tying each other up.

—ANN LANDERS

There's nothing better than good sex. But bad sex? A peanut butter and jelly sandwich is better than bad sex.

—BILLY JOEL

I like sex as much as I love music, and I think it's as hard to do.

—LINDA RONSTADT

Nuns are sexy.

—MADONNA

If a woman thinks she's sexy, she is.

—BURT REYNOLDS

I mean if I were out there in the desert and I'd no one to do it with, I still wouldn't do it with girls.

—KAREN BLACK,
American actress

Being good in bed means I'm propped up with my pillows and my mom brings me soup.

—BROOKE SHIELDS

I don't think you can take it too serious. Oh, it's very flattering—but the sexiest man alive . . . ? There are few sexy dead ones.

—SEAN CONNERY

Perhaps one can be a sex symbol when one is 20. There's insolence, youth, a certain lack of confidence. But at 40—it would be a remarkable sadness.

—GERARD DEPARDIEU

I regret three one-night stands—no, make that four.

—ANGIE DICKINSON

I believe that sex is one of the most beautiful, natural, wholesome things that money can buy.

—STEVE MARTIN

Masturbation: the primary sexual activity of mankind. In the nineteenth century it was a disease; in the twentieth, it's a cure.

—THOMAS SZASZ,
American psychiatrist

Don't knock masturbation. It's sex with someone I love.

—WOODY ALLEN,
in Annie Hall, *1977*

If homosexuality were the normal way, God would have made Adam and Bruce.

—ANITA BRYANT

You'll have to ask someone older than me.

—EUBIE BLAKE,
American jazz pianist and composer, when asked at the age of 97 when the sex drive goes

Certainly nothing is unnatural that is not physically impossible.

—RICHARD BRINSLEY SHERIDAN,
18th-century English playwright

The sexual embrace can only be compared with music and with prayer.

> —HAVELOCK ELLIS,
> *English sex researcher*

When you put a man and a woman together, there are some things they simply have to do. They embrace. They warm each other. All the rest is dead and empty.

> —UGO BETTI,
> *Italian writer*

One of the paramount reasons for staying attractive is so you can have somebody to go to bed with.

> —HELEN GURLEY BROWN

Men aren't attracted to my mind, they're attracted to what *I don't* mind.

> —GYPSY ROSE LEE,
> *American entertainer*

Love and sex can go together and sex and unlove can go together and love and unsex can go together. But personal love and personal sex is bad.

> —ANDY WARHOL

I make it a policy never to have sex before the first
date.

—SALLY FIELD

Sex is nobody's business except the three people
involved.

—ANONYMOUS

Sex is good, but not as good as fresh sweet corn.

—GARRISON KEILLOR

If God wanted sex to be fun, he wouldn't have
included children as punishment.

—ED BLUESTONE,
American humorist

Vasectomy means never having to say you're sorry.

—ANONYMOUS

When I think of some of the men I've slept with—
if they were women, I wouldn't have had lunch
with them.

—CAROL SISKIND,
Comedian

I have so little sex appeal that my gynecologist calls me "sir."

—JOAN RIVERS

I almost got a girl pregnant in high school. It's costing me a fortune to keep the rabbit on a life support system.

—WILL SHRINER,
American comedian

The cable TV sex channels don't expand our horizons, don't make us better people, and don't come in clearly enough.

—BILL MAHER

There is need of variety in sex, but not in love.

—THEODOR REIK,
Austrian psychologist

There's probably no sensitive heterosexual alive who is not preoccupied with his latent homosexuality.

—NORMAN MAILER

Making love is a mental illness that wastes time and energy.

> —PEOPLE'S REPUBLIC OF CHINA,
>   *Official Communist Party Proclamation, 1971*

The only reason you're still alive is that I never kissed you.

> —CHARLES DURNING,
>   *to Dustin Hoffman, in* Tootsie, *1982*

Sex is the biggest nothing of all time.

> —ANDY WARHOL

The pleasure is momentary, the position ridiculous, and the expense damnable.

> —LORD CHESTERFIELD,
>   *18th-century English politician and writer*

Why should we take advice on sex from the Pope? If he knows anything about it, he shouldn't.

> —GEORGE BERNARD SHAW

Sex is like money; only too much is enough.

> —JOHN UPDIKE

The highest level of sexual excitement is in a monogamous relationship.

—WARREN BEATTY

Sex is the last refuge of the miserable.

—QUENTIN CRISP,
English writer and humorist

What makes a woman good in bed? I would say a man who is good in bed.

—BOB GUCCIONNE,
American publisher

You know how Americans are when it comes to sex: the men can't keep from lying, and the women can't keep from telling the truth.

—ROBIN ZANDER,
of the band Cheap Trick

To the Latin, sex is an hors d'oeuvre; to the Anglo-Saxon, it is a barbecue.

—GEORGE JEAN NATHAN,
American editor, writer, and critic

Of the delights of this world man cares most for sexual intercourse, yet he has left it out of his heaven.

—MARK TWAIN

After coitus every animal is sad, except the rooster and the human female.

—GALEN,
1st-century Greek physician

Some things are better than sex, and some things are worse, but there's nothing exactly like it.

—W. C. FIELDS

The good thing about masturbation is that you don't have to get dressed up for it.

—TRUMAN CAPOTE

Sex hasn't been the same since women started enjoying it.

—LEWIS GRIZZARD,
Columnist

When sex is good, it's 10 percent of the relationship. When it's bad, it's 90 percent.

—CHARLES MUIR,
English writer and broadcaster

Sex is a conversation carried out by other means.

—PETER USTINOV

Is sex dirty? Only if it's done right.

—WOODY ALLEN

My brain: it's my second favorite organ.

—WOODY ALLEN,
in Sleeper, *1977*

If sex is such a natural phenomenon, how come there are so many books on how to?

—BETTE MIDLER

Whoever named it necking was a poor judge of anatomy.

—GROUCHO MARX

Sex is one of the nine reasons for reincarnation. The other eight are unimportant.

> —HENRY MILLER

Tell him I've been too fucking busy—or vice versa.

> —DOROTHY PARKER,
> *to her editor, on why her copy was late*

Really, sex and laughter do go very well together and I wondered—and still do—which is the more important.

> —HERMIONE GINGOLD,
> *Actress*

Sex Is Never an Emergency

> —TITLE OF BOOK BY ELAINE PIERSON

Sexuality is the great field of battle between biology and society.

> —NANCY FRIDAY,
> *American writer*

Despite a lifetime of service to the cause of sexual liberation, I have never caught a venereal disease, which makes me feel rather like an arctic explorer who has never had frostbite.

> —GERMAINE GREER,
> *English reformer and writer*

In America sex is an obsession, in other parts of the world it is a fact.

> —MARLENE DIETRICH

It has to be admitted that we English have sex on the brain, which is a very unsatisfactory place to have it.

> —MALCOLM MUGGERIDGE,
> *English editor and writer*

The more sex becomes a non-issue in people's lives, the happier they are.

> —SHIRLEY MACLAINE

A fast word about oral contraception: I asked a girl to go to bed with me and she said "no."

> —WOODY ALLEN

He said it was artificial respiration, but now I find I am to have his child.

—ANTHONY BURGESS,
English writer, in Inside Mr. Enderby

The big difference between sex for money and sex for free is that sex for money usually costs a lot less.

—BRENDAN BEHAN,
Irish playwright

In my sex fantasy, no one ever loves me for my mind.

—NORA EPHRON,
American writer

The possibilities of heterosexuality are very nearly exhausted.

—ANONYMOUS

Anyone who was seduced wanted to be seduced.

—MARLENE DIETRICH

The man-woman thing is a boring subject. It's
essentially a dead end. It's going to come down to one
of two things: either you're going to take your
clothes off or you're not.

> —Nikki Giovanni,
> *American writer*

She's descended from a long line her mother
listened to.

> —Gypsy Rose Lee,
> *American entertainer*

Older women are best because they always think they
may be doing it for the last time.

> —Ian Fleming

Sex is the poor man's polo.

> —Clifford Odets,
> *American playwright*

If your sexual fantasies were truly of interest to
others, they would no longer be fantasies.

> —Fran Lebowitz

Sex: the thing that takes up the least amount of time and causes the most amount of trouble.

—JOHN BARRYMORE

All this fuss about sleeping together. For physical pleasure I'd sooner go to my dentist any day.

—EVELYN WAUGH

Women liked me because I made them laugh. And what is an orgasm, except laughter of the loins?

—MICKEY ROONEY

Sex has become one of the most discussed subjects of modern times. The Victorians pretended it did not exist; the moderns pretend that nothing else exists.

—ARCHBISHOP FULTON J. SHEEN

Power is the great aphrodisiac.

—HENRY KISSINGER

Sex is too wonderful to be shared with anyone else.

—PHILLIP LARKIN,
    English poet

Any good whore knows more about sex than Betty
Friedan.

> —SAM PECKINPAH,
> *American film director*

Who sleeps with whom is intrinsically more
interesting than who votes for whom.

> —MALCOLM MUGGERIDGE,
> *English editor and writer*

I like sex and I don't care what a man thinks of me as
long as I get what I want from him—which is usually
sex.

> —VALERIE PERRINE,
> *American actress*

Dancing is the perpendicular expression of a
horizontal desire.

> —ANONYMOUS

I don't see so much of Alfred anymore since he got so
interested in sex.

> —CLARA KINSEY,
> *Wife of American sexologist Alfred Kinsey*

I think the people who like sex stay home. I mean I don't think they make a big thing out of it.

—NELSON ALGREN,
American writer

You're not supposed to mention fucking in mixed company, and yet that's precisely the place you're supposed to do it.

—GEORGE CARLIN

The fact is there hasn't been a thrilling new erogenous zone since de Sade.

—GEORGE GILDER,
American writer

If you aren't going all the way, why go at all?

—JOE NAMATH

I've got nothing against sex, it's a marvelous human activity, but it was watching others do it all the time that got me down.

—JOHN TREVELEYAN,
Former English film censor

I keep making all these sex rules for myself and then I break them right away.

> —HOLDEN CAULFIELD,
> *In J. D. Salinger's* Catcher in the Rye

What holds the world together, I have learned from bitter experience, is sexual intercourse.

> —HENRY MILLER

Murder is a crime. Describing murder is not. Sex is not a crime. Describing sex is.

> —GERSHON LEGMAN,
> *American writer*

The only known aphrodisiac is variety.

> —MARC CONNOLLY,
> *Essayist*

Sex in France is a comedy; in England it is a tragedy; in America it's a melodrama; in Italy it's an opera; in Germany, a reason to take up philosophy.

> —ANONYMOUS

Love between the sexes is a sin in theology, a
forbidden intercourse in jurisprudence, a mechanical
insult in medicine, and a subject philosophy has no
time for.

> —KARL KRAUS,
> *Austrian poet and journalist*

[Sex is] the last important human activity not subject
to taxation.

> —RUSSELL BAKER,
> *American humorist*

Sex touches the heavens only when it simultaneously
touches the gutter and the mud.

> —GEORGE JEAN NATHAN,
> *American editor, writer, and critic*

When grown-ups do it it's kind of dirty—that's
because there's no one to punish them.

> —TUESDAY WELD,
> *American actress*

A movie without sex would be like a candy bar without nuts.

> —EARL WILSON,
> *American columnist*

Why resist temptation—there will always be more.

> —DON HEROLD,
> *American writer and humorist*

In Europe men and woman have intercourse because they love each other. In the South Seas, they love each other because they have had intercourse. Who is right?

> —PAUL GAUGUIN

I'm saving the bass player for Omaha.

> —JANIS JOPLIN

Outside of every thin woman is a fat man trying to get in.

> —KATHERINE WHITEHORN,
> *English writer*

I sleep with men and with women. I am neither queer nor not queer, nor am I bisexual.

—ALLEN GINSBERG

Sex is a subject like any other subject. Every bit as interesting as agriculture.

—MURIEL SPARK,
Scottish writer

Thunder and lightning, wars, fires, plagues, have not done that mischief to mankind as this burning lust.

—ROBERT BURTON,
English clergyman and writer, in 1621

Leaving sex to the feminists is like letting your dog vacation at the taxidermist.

—CAMILLE PAGLIA

There is nothing safe about sex. There never will be.

—NORMAN MAILER

I know sex does make people happy, but to me it's just like having a cup of tea.

—CYNTHIA PAYNE,
English housewife, in 1987, after her acquittal for running a prostitution ring

If sex is a war, I am a conscientious objector: I will not play.

—MARGE PIERCY,
American writer

You don't need a Harvard MBA to know that the bedroom and the boardroom are just two sides of the same ballgame.

—STEPHEN FRY,
English comedy actor

There is no unhappier creature on earth than a fetishist, who yearns to embrace a woman's shoe and has to embrace the whole woman.

—KARL KRAUS,
Austrian poet and journalist

To talk about adults without talking about their sex drives is like talking about a window without glass.

—GRACE METALIOUS,
American writer

A sex symbol becomes a thing. I hate being a thing.

—MARILYN MONROE

Anyone who eats three meals a day should understand why cookbooks outsell sex books three to one.

—L. M. BOYD,
Columnist for the Seattle Post-Intelligencer

I think there are two areas where new ideas are terribly dangerous—economics and sex. By and large, it's all been tried before, and if it's new, it's probably illegal or unhealthy.

—FELIX ROHATYN,
American businessman

It is not sex that gives the pleasure, but the lover.

—MARGE PIERCY,
American writer

It's intoxicating for a man to be waited on. Combine this with very, very skillful sex, and that will get them.

—DORIS LILLY,
American journalist

Lifestyles and sex roles are passed from parents to children as inexorably as blue eyes or small feet.

—LETTY COTTIN POGREBIN,
American writer

Literature is mostly about sex and not much about having children and life is the other way around.

—DAVID LODGE,
English writer

Love is the answer, but while you're waiting for the answer, sex raises some pretty good questions.

—WOODY ALLEN

Sex appeal is the keynote of our civilization.

—HENRI BERGSON,
19th-century French philosopher

Talking from morning to night about sex has helped my skiing, because I talk about movement, about looking good, about taking risks.

—Dr. Ruth Westheimer

The Englishman can get along with sex quite perfectly so long as he can pretend that it isn't sex but something else.

—James Agate,
English critic and writer

The ability to make love frivolously is the thing that distinguishes human beings from beasts.

—Heywood C. Broun,
American journalist

The mind can also be an erogenous zone.

—Raquel Welch

The resistance of a woman is not always proof of her virtue but more frequently of her experience.

—Ninon de Lenclos,
17th-century French courtesan

There are two things people want more than sex and money—recognition and praise.

—MARY KAY ASH,
American businesswoman

There comes a moment in the day when you have written your pages in the morning, attended to your correspondence in the afternoon, and have nothing further to do. Then comes that hour when you are bored; that's the time for sex.

—H. G. WELLS

To my mind, the two most fascinating subjects in the universe are sex and the eighteenth century.

—BRIGID BROPHY,
English-Irish writer

To speak of morals in art is to speak of legislature in sex. Art is the sex of the imagination.

—GEORGE JEAN NATHAN,
American editor, writer, and critic

When I was young, I used to have successes with women because I was young. Now I have successes with women because I am old. Middle age was the hardest part.

—ARTUR RUBINSTEIN,
Polish-American pianist

When it comes to finances, remember that there are no withholding taxes on the wages of sin.

—MAE WEST

A kiss is a lovely trick designed by nature to stop speech when words become superfluous.

—INGRID BERGMAN

The only unnatural sex act is that which you cannot perform.

—ALFRED KINSEY

The total deprivation of it produces irritability.

—ELIZABETH BLACKWELL,
in The Human Element in Sex, *1894*

Chastity: the most unnatural of the sexual perversions.

> —ALDOUS HUXLEY,
> *English writer*

Chastity always takes its toll. In some it produces pimples; in others, sex laws.

> —KARL KRAUS,
> *Austrian poet and journalist*

Complete abstinence is easier than perfect moderation.

> —AUGUSTINE,
> *4th-century philosopher and religious figure*

7

TAKING THE PLUNGE

Marriage—Husbands—Wives—
Weddings—Fidelity

I love being married. It's so great to find
that one special person you want to
annoy for the rest of your life.

—RITA RUDNER

Marriage

The dread of loneliness is greater than the fear of bondage, so we get married.

> —CYRIL CONNOLLY,
> *English journalist and editor*

When a girl marries she exchanges the attentions of many men for the inattention of one.

> —HELEN ROWLAND,
> *English-American writer*

A successful man is one who makes as much as his wife can spend. A successful woman is one who can find such a man.

> —LANA TURNER

I've never been married or had a child, but I want that—very badly . . . Do you know anybody?

> —DIANNE WIEST

Strong women only marry weak men.

> —BETTE DAVIS

I hate work. That's why I got married.

> —Peg Bundy,
> *on "Married with Children"*

I remember after I got that marriage license I went across from the license bureau to a bar for a drink. The bartender said, "What'll you have, sir?" And I said, "A glass of hemlock."

> —Ernest Hemingway

Marriage is like a bank account. You put it in, you take it out, you lose interest.

> —Variously attributed

The first part of our marriage was very happy. But then, on the way back from the ceremony . . .

> —Henny Youngman,
> *American comedian*

If you want to know about a man you can find out an awful lot by looking at who he married.

> —Kirk Douglas

I don't worry about terrorism. I was married for two years.

—SAM KINISON

I've been married so long, I'm on my third bottle of Tabasco sauce.

—SUSAN VASS,
Writer and humorist

I was so cold the other day, I nearly got married.

—SHELLEY WINTERS

Many a man in love with a dimple makes the mistake of marrying the whole girl.

—STEPHEN LEACOCK,
Canadian economist and humorist

Every woman should marry, and no man.

—BENJAMIN DISRAELI,
19th-century English writer and statesman

LADY ASTOR: If you were my husband, Winston, I'd
   put poison in your tea.
WINSTON CHURCHILL: If I were your husband, Nancy,
   I'd drink it.

Show me one couple unhappy merely on account of
their limited circumstances, and I will show you ten
who are wretched from other causes.

> —SAMUEL TAYLOR COLERIDGE,
>   *English poet, critic, and essayist*

The men that women marry, and the women that
marry them, will always be a marvel and a mystery to
the world.

> —HENRY WADSWORTH LONGFELLOW

The real killer was when you married the wrong
person but had the right children.

> —ANN BEATTIE,
>   *American writer*

Marriage is like a hot bath. Once you get used to it,
it's not so hot.

> —ANONYMOUS

A successful marriage requires falling in love several times, always with the same person.

> —MIGNON MCLAUGHLIN,
> *American journalist*

Marriage is a romance in which the hero dies in the first chapter.

> —ANONYMOUS

Laugh and the world laughs with you. Snore and you sleep alone.

> —ANTHONY BURGESS,
> *English writer*

There is one thing more exasperating than a spouse who can cook and won't, and that is a spouse who can't cook and will.

> —ANONYMOUS

I've sometimes thought of marrying, and then I've thought again.

> —NOEL COWARD

I belong to Bridegrooms Anonymous. Whenever I feel like getting married, they send over a lady in a housecoat and hair curlers to burn my toast for me.

—DICK MARTIN

Married. It was like a dream come true for Donna. Just think, soon her little girl would have unpaid bills, unplanned babies, calls from the bank, and sub-standard housing. All the things a mother dreams of for her child.

—ERMA BOMBECK

What counts in making a happy marriage is not so much how compatible you are, but how you deal with incompatibility.

—GEORGE LEVINGER,
Essayist

The trouble with many married people is that they are trying to get more out of marriage than there is in it.

—ELBERT HUBBARD,
American writer

The appropriate age for marriage is about the
eighteenth year for girls and for men the thirty-
seventh year, plus or minus.

—Aristotle

By 1975 sexual feeling and marriage will have nothing
to do with each other.

—John Langdon-Davies,
Anthropologist, in 1936

I am about to be married—and am of course in all the
misery of a man in pursuit of happiness.

—Lord Byron

Though familiarity may not breed contempt, it takes
off the edge of admiration.

—William Hazlitt,
19th-century English writer

It is better to marry than to burn.

—The Bible,
1 Corinthians 7:9

No man is regular in his attendance at the House of Commons until he is married.

—BENJAMIN DISRAELI,
19th-century English writer and statesman

If I ever marry it will be on a sudden impulse, as a man shoots himself.

—H. L. MENCKEN,
American editor and satirist

Ideally, couples need three lives; one for him, one for her, and one for them together.

—JACQUELINE BISSET

My wife and I tried to breakfast together, but we had to stop or our marriage would have been wrecked.

—WINSTON CHURCHILL

I hated my marriage, but I always had a great place to park.

—GERALD NACHMAN,
Writer

Nothing anybody tells you about marriage helps.

—MAX SIEGEL

I'd like to get married because I like the idea of a man being required by law to sleep with me every night.

—CARRIE SNOW,
Comedian

I was married by a judge. I should have asked for a jury.

—GEORGE BURNS

Marriage is really tough because you have to deal with feelings and lawyers.

—RICHARD PRYOR

If you want to read about love and marriage, you've got to buy two separate books.

—ALAN KING

Why did you two ever get married?

Ah, I don't know. It was raining, and we were in
    Pittsburgh.

> —BARBARA STANWYCK AND HELEN BRODERICK,
> *in* The Bride Walks Out, *1936*

The most happy marriage I can imagine . . . would be
the union of a deaf man to a blind woman.

> —SAMUEL TAYLOR COLERIDGE,
> *English poet, critic, and essayist*

The surest way to be alone is to get married.

> —GLORIA STEINEM

I couldn't see tying myself down to a middle-aged
woman with four children, even though the woman
was my wife and the children were my own.

> —JOSEPH HELLER

The only really happy folk are married women and
single men.

> —H. L. MENCKEN,
> *American editor and satirist*

Marriage probably originated as a food-for-sex deal among foraging primates. Compatibility was not a big issue, nor, of course, was there any tension over who would control the remote.

—BARBARA EHRENREICH,
American writer

One was never married, and that's his hell; another is, and that's his plague.

—ROBERT BURTON,
17th-century English writer and clergyman

Take it from me, marriage isn't a word . . . it's a sentence!

—VARIOUSLY ATTRIBUTED

Those who are outside want to get in, and those who are inside want to get out.

—ANONYMOUS

The bonds of matrimony are like any other bonds—they mature slowly.

—PETER DEVRIES,
American writer and humorist

The great secret of successful marriage is to treat all disasters as incidents, and none of the incidents as disasters.

—HAROLD NICOLSON,
English diplomat and writer

When should a man marry?
A young man not yet, an elder man not at all.

—THALES,
6th- and 7th-century B.C. Greek philosopher and scientist

Marry in haste, and repent at leisure.

—PROVERB

You know that the urge for revenge is a fact of marital life.

—JANE SMILEY

Happiness in marriage is entirely a matter of chance.

—JANE AUSTEN,
from Pride and Prejudice

We can't get married at all . . . I'm a man.

Well, nobody's perfect.

>—Jack Lemmon (as Daphne) to Joe E. Brown
>(as Osgood Fielding),
>*in* Some Like It Hot, *1959*

Keep thy eyes wide open before marriage, half-shut afterwards.

>—Benjamin Franklin

Marriage is neither Heaven nor Hell. It is simply Purgatory.

>—Abraham Lincoln,
>*Attributed*

Marriage is the only evil men pray for.

>—Greek proverb

I've married a few people I shouldn't have, but haven't we all?

>—Mamie Van Doren,
>*American actress*

Marriage is a wonderful invention; but then again so is a bicycle repair kit.

>—BILLY CONNOLLY,
>*English comedian*

It destroys one's nerves to be amiable every day to the same human being.

>—BENJAMIN DISRAELI,
>*19th-century English writer and statesman*

One fool at least in every married couple.

>—HENRY FIELDING,
>*18th-century English writer*

The critical period in matrimony is breakfast time.

>—A. P. HERBERT,
>*English writer and politician*

Most marriages don't add two people together. They subtract one from the other.

>—IAN FLEMING

When you're bored with yourself, marry and be bored with someone else.

—DAVID PRYCE-JONES,
English humorist

Many a good hanging prevents a bad marriage.

—WILLIAM SHAKESPEARE,
from Twelfth Night

Marriage is a great institution, but I'm not ready for an institution yet.

—MAE WEST

The most difficult year of marriage is the one you're in.

—FRANKLIN P. JONES,
American businessman

It is always incomprehensible to a man that a woman should ever refuse an offer of marriage.

—JANE AUSTEN

Marriage is the only war where one sleeps with the enemy.

—Mexican proverb

Marriage always demands the finest arts of insincerity possible between two human beings.

—Vicki Baum,
American writer

I've had an exciting life. I married for love and got a little money along with it.

—Rose Fitzgerald Kennedy

Sexiness wears thin after a while and beauty fades, but to be married to a man who makes you laugh everyday, ah, now that's a real treat!

—Joanne Woodward

Husbands

Bigamy is having one husband too many. Monogamy is the same.

—Erica Jong

Husbands never become good, they merely become proficient.

—H. L. MENCKEN,
American editor and satirist

I think every woman's entitled to a middle husband she can forget.

—ADELA ROGERS ST. JOHNS,
American reporter

Behind every successful man stands a surprised mother-in-law.

—HUBERT HUMPHREY

American women expect to find in their husbands a perfection that English women only expect to find in their butlers.

—W. SOMERSET MAUGHAM,
English writer

The husband who wants a happy marriage should learn to keep his mouth shut and his checkbook open.

—GROUCHO MARX

A woman never knows what kind of husband she doesn't want until she marries him.

　　—ANONYMOUS

I won't say my previous husbands thought only of my money, but it did hold a certain fascination for them.

　　—BARBARA HUTTON,
　　American heiress

A man finds himself seven years older the day after his marriage.

　　—FRANCIS BACON,
　　English philosopher and statesman

My husband's going through a mid-life crisis. He left me for an older woman! What does she have that I don't, except osteoporosis and orthopedic shoes? If he would've waited ten years, I could have given him those.

　　—EILEEN FINNEY,
　　Actress

A man would prefer to come home to an unmade bed and a happy woman than to a neatly made bed and an angry woman.

—MARLENE DIETRICH

All men make mistakes, but married men find out about them sooner.

—RED SKELTON

Marriage to a lover is fatal; lovers are not husbands. More important, husbands are not lovers. The compulsion to find a lover and husband in a single person has doomed more women to misery than any other illusion.

—CAROLYN HEILBURN,
American writer

The majority of husbands remind me of an orangutan trying to play the violin.

—HONORÉ DE BALZAC,
19th-century French writer

A husband should not insult his wife publicly, at parties. He should insult her in the privacy of the home.

—JAMES THURBER,
   American writer and humorist

Positive reinforcement is hugging your husband when he does a load of laundry. Negative reinforcement is telling him he used too much detergent.

—DR. JOYCE BROTHERS

I think men who have a pierced ear are better prepared for marriage. They've experienced pain and bought jewelry.

—RITA RUDNER

Why does a woman work ten years to change a man's habits and then complain that he's not the man she married?

—BARBRA STREISAND

A wife should tell her husband in clear, simple language, where guest towels come from.

—JAMES THURBER AND E. B. WHITE

No man, examining his marriage intelligently, can fail to observe that it is compounded, at least in part, of slavery, and that he is the slave.

> —H. L. MENCKEN,
> *American editor and satirist*

It's no disgrace for a woman to make a mistake in marrying—every woman does it.

> —EDGAR WATSON HOWE,
> *19th-century American writer and editor*

There are no father-in-law jokes.

> —ANONYMOUS

Wives

Bigamy is having one wife too many. Monogamy is the same.

> —OSCAR WILDE

My wife's jealousy is getting ridiculous. The other day she looked at my calendar and wanted to know who May was.

> —RODNEY DANGERFIELD

After a man is married he has the legal right to deceive only one woman.

> —EDGAR WATSON HOWE,
> *19th-century American writer and editor*

Marriage is a bribe to make a housekeeper think she's a householder.

> —THORNTON WILDER

No man should marry until he has studied anatomy and dissected at least one woman.

> —HONORÉ DE BALZAC,
> *19th-century French writer*

Choose a wife rather by your ear than your eye.

> —THOMAS FULLER, M.D.,
> *17th- and 18th-century English physician and writer*

When a man opens the car door for his wife, it's either a new car or a new wife.

> —PRINCE PHILIP,
> *Duke of Edinburgh*

All married women are not wives.

—Japanese proverb

The trouble with my wife is that she's a whore in the kitchen and a cook in bed.

—Geoffrey Gorer,
English writer and anthropologist

The others were only my wives. But you, my dear, will be my widow.

—Sacha Guitry,
French actor and playwright

If you want to find out some things about yourself— and in vivid detail, too—just try calling your wife 'fat.'

—P. J. O'Rourke,
American journalist and humorist

If you want all the world to know, tell your wife.

—Estonian proverb

A wife isn't a mitten—you can't take her off your hand.

>   —RUSSIAN PROVERB

By all means marry: if you get a good wife you'll become happy; if you get a bad one, you'll become a philosopher.

>   —SOCRATES

Any woman who reads the marriage contract, and then goes into it, deserves all the consequences.

>   —ISADORA DUNCAN,
>   *American dancer*

The comfortable estate of widowhood is the only hope that keeps up a wife's spirits.

>   —JOHN GAY,
>   *18th-century English poet and playwright*

If men knew how women pass the time when they are alone, they'd never marry.

>   —O. HENRY

My wife doesn't. Understand me?

> —WILLIAM COLE,
> *American writer and editor*

My wife thinks I'm too nosy. At least that's what she keeps scribbling in her diary.

> —DRAKE SATHER,
> *Comedian*

Here lies my wife; here let her lie!
Now she's at rest, and so am I.

> —JOHN DRYDEN,
> *Intended epitaph for his wife*

A psychiatrist asks a lot of expensive questions your wife asks for nothing.

> —JOEY ADAMS,
> *Humorist*

My toughest fight was with my first wife.

> —MUHAMMAD ALI

A good wife is good, but the best wife is not so good as no wife at all.

> —THOMAS HARDY

To want a wife is better than to need one, especially if it happens to be your neighbor's.

> —NORMAN DOUGLAS,
> *English writer*

Maybe today's successful marriage is when a man is in love with his wife and only one other woman.

> —MATT BASILE,
> *American private detective*

Every man should have two wives: one to cook for him, and another to amuse him after he has eaten.

> —EDGAR WATSON HOWE,
> *19th-century American writer and editor*

I know a mother-in-law who sleeps with her glasses on, the better to see her son-in-law suffer in her dreams.

> —ERNEST COQUELIN,
> *19th-century French comic actor*

Men's wives are usually their husband's mental inferiors and spiritual superiors; this gives them double instruments of torture.

—DON HEROLD,
American writer and humorist

In Biblical times, a man could have as many wives as he could afford. Just like today.

—ABIGAIL VAN BUREN

Never feel remorse for what you have thought about your wife. She has thought much worse things about you.

—JEAN ROSTAND,
French biologist and writer

I have more than enough of a wife in my art.

—MICHELANGELO

A sweetheart is a bottle of wine; a wife is a wine bottle.

—CHARLES-PIERRE BAUDELAIRE,
19th-century French poet

Only two things are necessary to keep one's wife happy. One is to let her think she is having her own way, and the other, to let her have it.

—LYNDON B. JOHNSON

A sweetheart is milk, a bride is butter, and a wife—is cheese.

—LUDWIG BOERNE,
German writer

After seven years of marriage, I'm sure of two things. First, never wallpaper together, and second, you'll need two bathrooms. Both for her.

—DENNIS MILLER

The only time some fellows are seen with their wives is after they've been indicted.

—KIN HUBBARD,
American journalist and humorist

My wife doesn't care what I do while I'm away as long as I don't have a good time.

—LEE TREVINO

She'd have you spew up what you've drunk when you were out.

—CAECILIUS,
1st-century Greek rhetorician

Marriage is traditionally the destiny offered to women by society. Most women are married or have been, or plan to be or suffer from not being.

—SIMONE DE BEAUVOIR,
French writer

Nobody works as hard for his money as the man who marries it.

—KIN HUBBARD,
American journalist and humorist

Weddings

Girls usually have a papier-mâché face on their wedding day.

—COLETTE,
French writer

If it were not for the presents, an elopement would be preferable.

>—GEORGE ADE,
> *American humorist and playwright*

Brides aren't happy—they're just triumphant.

>—JOHN BARRYMORE

The music at a wedding procession always reminds me of the music of soldiers going into battle.

>—HEINRICH HEINE,
> *19th-century German poet*

The most dangerous food is wedding cake.

>—AMERICAN PROVERB

Niagara Falls is only the second biggest disappointment of the standard honeymoon.

>—OSCAR WILDE

Fidelity

If you were married to Marilyn Monroe, you'd cheat with some ugly girl.

—GEORGE BURNS

Some people claim that marriage interferes with romance. There's no doubt about it. Anytime you have a romance, your wife is bound to interfere.

—GROUCHO MARX

Honesty has ruined more marriages than infidelity.

—CHARLES MCCABE,
American writer

Eighty percent of married men cheat in America. The rest cheat in Europe.

—JACKIE MASON

My wife was in labor with our first child for thirty-two hours and I was faithful to her the whole time.

—JONATHAN KATZ,
Writer and humorist

A hundred years ago Hester Prynne of *The Scarlet Letter* was given an A for Adultery; today she would rate no better than a C plus.

> —PETER DEVRIES,
> *American writer and humorist*

I say I don't sleep with married men, but what I mean is that I don't sleep with happily married men.

> —BRITT EKLAND

Adultery is the application of democracy to love.

> —H. L. MENCKEN,
> *American writer and humorist*

Monogamy is impossible these days for both sexes. I don't know anyone who's faithful or wants to be.

> —GOLDIE HAWN

A man can have two, maybe three love affairs while he's married. After that it's cheating.

> —YVES MONTAND

Marriage has driven more than one man to sex.

> —PETER DEVRIES

I wouldn't trust my husband with a young woman for five minutes, and he's been dead for 25 years.

—IRISH PLAYWRIGHT BRENDAN BEHAN'S MOTHER

Adultery is like dung; one goes far to do it.

—AFRICAN PROVERB

Were all the adulterers to wear gray coats, the cloth would be expensive.

—GERMAN PROVERB

Prostitutes believe in marriage. It provides them with most of their trade.

—ANONYMOUS

When cheated, wife or husband feels the same.

—EURIPIDES

I'm not a real movie star—I still got the same wife I started out with nearly 28 years ago.

—WILL ROGERS

8

MUCH "I DO" ABOUT NOTHING

Divorce, Alimony, and Remarriage

Divorce is the sacrament of adultery.

—FRENCH PROVERB

The desire for divorce is the only important factor.
The reasons do not matter.

—Heywood C. Broun,
American journalist

Some couples divorce because of a misunderstanding;
others, because they understand each other too well.

—Evan Esar,
American editor

I'd marry again if I found a man who had
$15,000,000, would sign over half of it to me before
the marriage, and guarantee he'd be dead within a
year.

—Bette Davis

Alimony: Disinterest, compounded annually.

—Walter McDonald,
American poet

A wife lasts only for the length of the marriage, but
an ex-wife is there for the rest of your life.

—Woody Allen

Many a man owes his success to his first wife and his second wife to his success.

—JIM BACKUS

It wasn't exactly a divorce—I was traded.

—TIM CONWAY

Judges, as a class, display, in the matter of arranging alimony, that reckless generosity which is found only in men who are giving away someone else's cash.

—P. G. WODEHOUSE,
English writer and humorist

She cried, and the judge wiped her tears with my checkbook.

—TOMMY MANVILLE,
Writer

You don't know anything about a woman until you meet her in court.

—NORMAN MAILER

Half of all marriages end in divorce—and then there are the real unhappy ones.

—JOAN RIVERS

Alimony: The cash surrender value of the American male.

—ANONYMOUS

So many persons think divorce is a panacea for every ill, who find out, when they try it, that the remedy is worse than the disease.

—DOROTHEA DIX,
American journalist

If you feel like getting a divorce, you are no exception to the general rule.

—ELIZABETH HAWES,
Writer

What a holler would ensue if people had to pay the minister as much to marry them as they have to pay a lawyer to get them a divorce.

—CLAIRE TREVOR,
Actress

I married twice. The first time was to prove to my mother that I could.

> —MEREDITH TAX,
> *Writer*

My divorce came as a complete surprise to me. This will happen when you haven't been home in eighteen years.

> —LEE TREVINO

Changing husbands is only changing troubles.

> —KATHLEEN NORRIS,
> *American writer*

A wife is a person who reminds you that her allowance is not as big as her alimony would be.

> —VAUGHN MONROE,
> *American band leader*

Divorce is fission after fusion.

> —RITA MAE BROWN

There are three sides to every question—where a divorce is involved.

—ELBERT HUBBARD,
American writer

Divorce is a game played by lawyers.

—CARY GRANT

Alimony is the most exorbitant of all stud-fees, and the worst feature of it is that you pay it retroactively.

—JOHN BARRYMORE

Paying alimony is like feeding hay to a dead horse.

—GROUCHO MARX

The happiest time in anyone's life is just after the first divorce.

—JOHN KENNETH GALBRAITH,
American economist, author, and diplomat

One of the surest signs that a woman is in love is when she divorces her husband.

—DOLLY PARTON

One reason people get divorced is that they run out of gift ideas.

—ROBERT BYRNE,
American writer and editor

Marriage is like the army. Everybody complains, but you'd be surprised at how many people re-enlist.

—ANONYMOUS

Conrad Hilton was very generous to me in the divorce settlement. He gave me 5,000 Gideon Bibles.

—ZSA ZSA GABOR

Divorce is probably of nearly the same date as marriage. I believe, however, that marriage is some weeks more ancient.

—VOLTAIRE

American husbands are the best in the world; no other husbands are so generous to their wives, or can be so easily divorced.

—ELINOR GLYN,
English writer

Getting divorced just because you don't love a man is almost as silly as getting married just because you do.

—ZSA ZSA GABOR

I've given my memoirs far more thought than any of my marriages. You can't divorce a book.

—GLORIA SWANSON,
American actress, producer, and business executive

If income tax is the price you have to pay to keep the government on its feet, alimony is the price we have to pay for sweeping a woman off hers.

—GROUCHO MARX

In Hollywood, an equitable divorce settlement means each party getting fifty percent of publicity.

—LAUREN BACALL

I kept putting my wife under a pedestal.

—WOODY ALLEN,
on why his first marriage failed

Being married six times shows a degree of optimism over wisdom, but I am incorrigibly optimistic.

—NORMAN MAILER

My first wife divorced me on grounds of incompatibility—and besides, I think she hated me.

—OSCAR LEVANT,
American actor and writer

I was married once. Now I just lease.

—IN *BUDDY BUDDY*, 1981

In every marriage more than a week old, there are grounds for divorce. The trick is to find, and to continue to find, grounds for marriage.

—ROBERT ANDERSON,
American writer

He taught me housekeeping; when we divorce, I keep the house.

—ZSA ZSA GABOR

I don't think I'll get married again. I think I'll just find a woman I don't like and give her a house.

—LEWIS GRIZZARD,
Columnist

I don't see any reason for marriage when there is divorce.

—CATHERINE DENEUVE

Divorce: the result of much 'I do' about nothing.

—ANONYMOUS

I am never going to get divorced and that's that. Whatever people may think and say. I'm very happy, thank you very much.

—DIANA, PRINCESS OF WALES,
in 1991

Before you marry, make sure you know whom you're going to divorce.

—YIDDISH PROVERB

What scares me about divorce is that my children
might put me in a home for unwed mothers.

—TERESSA SKELTON,
Writer

You Americans all get divorced because you make
such a big deal of infidelity.

—ORSON BEAN,
Actor

The difference between divorce and legal separation
is that a legal separation gives a husband time to hide
his money.

—JOHNNY CARSON

A lot of people have asked me how short I am. Since
my last divorce, I think I'm about $100,000 short.

—MICKEY ROONEY

Divorce is my generation's coming of age
ceremony—a ritual scarring that makes anything that
happens afterward seem bearable.

—ERICA JONG

Divorces are made in heaven.

—Oscar Wilde

Divorce is the psychological equivalent of a triple coronary bypass.

—Mary Kay Blakely,
American writer

A divorce is like an amputation; you survive, but there's less of you.

—Margaret Atwood

A lawyer is never entirely comfortable with a friendly divorce, anymore than a good mortician wants to finish his job and then have the patient sit up on the table.

—Jean Kerr,
American writer and humorist

Bibliography

Andrews, Robert, ed. *The Concise Columbia Dictionary of Quotations*. New York: Columbia University Press, 1989.

———. *Famous Lines: A Columbia Dictionary of Familiar Quotations*. New York: Columbia University Press, 1997.

Augarde, Tony, ed. *The Oxford Dictionary of Modern Quotations*. New York: Oxford University Press, 1991.

Barkin, George, ed. *The Sardonic Humor of Ambrose Bierce*. New York: Dover, 1963.

Baron, Joseph L., ed. *A Treasury of Jewish Quotations*. Northvale, NJ: Jason Aronson, 1985.

Barry, Dave. *Dave Barry's Complete Guide to Guys*. New York: Random House, 1995.

Bell, Janet Cheatham, ed. *Famous Black Quotations*. New York: Warner Books, 1994.

Berger, John. *Ways of Seeing*. New York: Penguin, 1991.

Bierce, Ambrose. *The Devil's Dictionary*. New York: Dover, 1958.

Bohle, Bruce, ed. *The Home Book of American Quotations*. New York: Dodd, Mead & Company, 1967.

Bolander, Donald O., ed. *Instant Quotation Dictionary*. Danbury, CT: Franklin-Watts, 1986.

Brussell, Eugene E., ed. *Webster's New World Dictionary of Quotable Definitions*. 2nd ed. New York: Simon & Schuster, 1970.

Burke, John Gordon, and Ned Kehde, eds. *Dictionary of Contemporary Quotations*. 3rd rev. ed. John Gordon Burke Publishers, Inc., 1994.

Byrne, Robert, ed. *1,911 Best Things Anybody Ever Said*. New York: Fawcett, 1988.

Cerf, Christopher, and Victor S. Navasky. *The Experts Speak: The Definitive Compendium of Authoritative Misinformation*. New York: Villard, 1998.

Charlton, James, ed. *The Executive's Quotation Book*. New York: St. Martin's Press, 1993.

Cohen, J. M., and M. J. Cohen, eds. *The Penguin Dictionary of Modern Quotations*. 2nd ed. New York: Penguin, 1980.

Cole, William, and Louis Phillips, eds. *Sex: The Most Fun You Can Have Without Laughing*. Edison, NJ: Castle Books, 1997.

———. *Sex: Even More Fun You Can Have Without Laughing*. Edison, NJ: Castle Books, 1997.

Contradictory Quotations. Burnt Mill, England: Longman, 1983.

Crainer, Stuart, ed. *The Ultimate Book of Business Quotations*. New York: AMACOM, 1998.

Crawley, Tony, ed. *Chambers Film Quotes*. New York: Chambers, 1991.

Curruth, Gorton, and Eugene Ehrlich, eds. *The Giant Book of American Quotations*. New York: Portland House, 1988.

De Beauvoir, Simone. *The Second Sex*. New York: Vintage, 1974.

Donadio, Stephen, et al., eds. *The New York Public Library Book of 20th-Century Quotations*. New York: Warner, 1992.

Esar, Evan, ed. *20,000 Quips and Quotes*. New York: Doubleday, 1968.

Fadiman, Clifton, ed. *The Little, Brown Book of Anecdotes*. Boston: Little, Brown, 1985.

Fergusson, Rosalind, ed. *The Penguin Dictionary of Proverbs*. New York: Penguin, 1983.

Fitzhenry, Robert I., ed. *The Barnes & Noble Book of Quotations*. New York: Barnes & Noble, 1981.

Fleisch, Rudolf, ed. *The New Book of Unusual Quotations*. New York: Harper & Row, 1966.

Frank, Leonard Roy, ed. *Random House Webster's Quotationary*. New York: Random House, 1999.

Heimel, Cynthia. *If You Can't Live Without Me, Why Aren't You Dead Yet?* New York: HarperCollins, 1992.

Isaacs, Alan, ed. *Cassell Dictionary of Sex Quotations*. London: Market House Books, 1993.

James, Simon R., ed. *A Dictionary of Sexist Quotations.* New York: Barnes & Noble, 1984.

Jarman, Colin, ed. *The Guinness Book of Poisonous Quotes.* Lincolnwood, IL: Contemporary Books, 1991.

Keillor, Garrison. *The Book of Guys.* New York: Viking, 1993.

Knowles, Elizabeth, ed. *The Oxford Dictionary of Quotations.* 5th ed. New York: Oxford University Press, 1999.

Lansky, Bruce, ed. *Lovesick: The Best Quotations About Love and Sex.* New York: Meadowbrook Press, 1996.

Lebowitz, Fran. *Metropolitan Life.* New York: Dutton, 1978.

———. *Social Studies.* New York: Random House, 1981.

The MacMillan Dictionary of Quotations. New York: MacMillan, 1989.

McKenzie, Carole, ed. *Quotable Sex.* New York: St. Martin's, 1992.

McWilliams, Peter, ed. *The Life 101 Quote Book.* Los Angeles: Prelude Press, 1997.

Machale, Des, ed. *Wit: Humorous Quotations from Woody Allen to Oscar Wilde*. New York: Fine Communications, 1999.

Maggio, Rosalie, comp. *The Beacon Book of Quotations by Women*. Boston: Beacon Press, 1992.

Markoe, Merrill. *Merrill Markoe's Guide to Love*. New York: Grove/Atlantic, 1998.

Marsden, C. R. S., comp. *The Dictionary of Outrageous Quotations*. Topsfield, MA: Salem House, 1988.

Mieder, Wolfgang, ed. *The Prentice-Hall Encyclopedia of World Proverbs*. Englewood Cliffs, NJ: Prentice-Hall, 1986.

Murphy, Edward F., ed. *2,715 One-Line Quotations for Speakers, Writers and Raconteurs*. New York: Random House, 1989.

Newman, Amanda, ed. *Women Are from Venus, Men Are from Hell*. Holbrook, MA: Adams Media Corporation, 1999.

Nowlan, Robert A., and Gwendolyn W. Nowlan, eds. *Film Quotations*. Jefferson, NC: McFarland & Co., 1994.

O'Connor, Joey. *Women Are Always Right and Men Are Never Wrong*. Nashville, TN: Word Publishing, 1999.

Paglia, Camille. *Sex, Art, and American Culture*. New York: Vintage, 1992.

———. *Sexual Personae*. New York: Vintage, 1991.

Panati, Charles. *Sexy Origins and Intimate Things*. New York: Penguin, 1998.

Parker, Dorothy. *The Portable Dorothy Parker*. New York: Viking, 1973.

Partnow, Elaine, ed. *The Quotable Woman*. New York: Facts On File, 1992.

Peter, Laurence J., ed. *Peter's Quotations: Ideas for Our Time*. New York: William Morrow, 1977.

Petras, Kathryn, and Ross Petras, eds. *The Whole World Book of Quotations*. Reading, MA: Addison-Wesley, 1995.

Phillips, Louis, and William Cole., eds. *The Random House Treasury of Humorous Quotations*. New York: Random House, 1996.

Platt, Suzy, ed. *Respectfully Quoted: A Dictionary of Quotations from the Congressional Research Service.* Washington, DC: Library of Congress, U.S. Government Printing Office, 1989.

Porter, Dahlia, ed. *365 Reflections on Dating.* Holbrook, MA: Adams Media Corporation, 2000.

Quinn, Tracy, ed. *Quotable Women of the Twentieth Century.* New York: William Morrow, 1999.

The Quotable Woman. Philadelphia: Running Press, 1991.

Rando, Catarina, ed. *Words of Women: Quotations for Success.* San Francisco: Power Dynamics Publishing, 1995.

Rasmussen, R. Kent, ed. *The Quotable Mark Twain.* Lincolnwood, IL: Contemporary Books, 1997.

Ratcliffe, Susan, ed. *Oxford Love Quotations.* New York: Oxford University Press, 1999.

Rawson, Hugh, and Margaret Milner, eds. *A Dictionary of Quotations from Shakespeare.* New York: Penguin, 1996.

Rawson, Hugh, and Margaret Milner, eds. *The New International Dictionary of Quotations*. New York: E. P. Dutton, 1986.

Reed, Tina, and Robert Reed, eds. *Speaking of Marriage: Irreverent Thoughts on Matrimony*. New York: Perigee, 1995.

Rimler, Marlene, ed. *The Other Species: Observations on the Study of Men*. Glendale Heights, IL: Great Quotations, 1997.

Rosenberg, Helena Hacker. *How to Get Married After 35*. New York: HarperCollins, 1998

Seldes, George, comp. *The Great Quotations*. Secaucus, NJ: Citadel Press, 1983.

Sherrin, Ned, ed. *The Oxford Dictionary of Humorous Quotations*. New York: Oxford University Press, 1995.

Shipman, David. *Movie Talk: Who Said What to Whom in the Movies*. New York: St. Martin's, 1988.

Shwartz, Ronald B., ed. *The 501 Best and Worst Things Ever Said About Marriage*. New York: Citadel Press, 1995.

Simpson, James B., ed. *Simpson's Contemporary Quotations: The Most Notable Quotes from 1950 to the Present.* New York: HarperCollins, 1997.

Stephens, Autumn, ed. *Wild Words from Wild Women: An Unabridged Collection of Candid Observations and Extremely Opinionated Bon Mots.* Berkeley, CA: Conari Press, 1996.

Sumrall, Amber Coverdale, ed. *Write to the Heart: Wit & Wisdom of Women Writers.* Freedom, CA: Crossing Press, 1992.

Tannen, Deborah. *You Just Don't Understand: Women and Men in Conversation.* New York: William Morrow, 1990.

Thomsett, Michael C., and Jean Freestone Thomsett, eds. *Sex and Love Quotations: A Worldwide Dictionary of Pronouncements About Gender and Sexuality Throughout the Ages.* Jefferson, NC: McFarland & Co., 1995.

Thurber, James, and E. B. White. *Is Sex Necessary?* New York: Harper & Row, 1929.

Tilsner, Julie. *29 and Counting: A Chick's Guide to Turning 30.* Lincolnwood, IL: Contemporary Books, 1998.

Tomlinson, Gerald, ed. *Treasury of Religious Quotations*. Englewood Cliffs, NJ: Prentice-Hall, 1991.

Tripp, Rhoda Thomas, comp. *The International Thesaurus of Quotations*. New York: Harper & Row, 1970.

21st-Century Dictionary of Quotations. Edited by Princeton Language Institute. New York: Dell, 1993.

Warner, Carolyn, ed. *The Last Word: A Treasury of Women's Quotes*. Englewood Cliffs, NJ: Prentice-Hall, 1992.

Warren, Roz, ed. *The Women's Lip*. Naperville, IL: Sourcebooks, 1998.

Winokur, John, comp. *The Portable Curmudgeon*. New York: New American Library, 1989.

———. *Portable Curmudgeon Redux*. New York: Dutton, 1992.

Wurtzel, Elizabeth. *Bitch: In Praise of Difficult Women*. New York: Random House, 1999.

Index

Abel, Milt, 136
Abortion, 91
Abstinence, 165
Acton, William, 60
Adam and Eve, 5, 6, 12, 18, 20, 79
Adams, Abigail, 62
Adams, Cindy, 80
Adams, Joey, 192
Adams, John, 62
Addison, Joseph, 14
Ade, George, 197
Adultery, 20. *See also* Fidelity
Agate, James, 162
Aging, 7, 10, 32, 33, 35, 50, 90, 140
Alcott, Louisa May, 26, 93
Aleichem, Shalom, 99
Alexander, Shana, 80
Algren, Nelson, 134, 154
Ali, Muhammad, 192
Alimony, 202, 203, 204, 205, 206, 208
Allen, Tim, 121
Allen, Woody, 117, 140, 147, 149, 161,
    202, 208
Anderson, Robert, 209
Animals, 29, 68
Annie Hall (film), 140
Anorexia, 67

Aphrodisiacs, 153, 156
Appearance, 3, 4, 86, 87, 112. *See also*
    Beauty
Aristophenes, 51
Aristotle, 6, 174
Armour, Richard, 6
Arnold, Thomas, 103
Ash, Mary Kay, 163
Ashley, Elizabeth, 131
Astor, Lady, 171
Atkinson, Brooks, 116
Atkinson, Ti-Grace, 41
Atwood, Margaret, 212
Auchincloss, Louis, 103
Auden, W. H., 92
Augustine, 125, 165
Austen, Jane, 49, 50, 125, 179, 182
Automobiles, 42, 121

Bacall, Lauren, 208
Bachelors, 98–100
Backus, Jim, 203
Bacon, Francis, 100, 185
Bad women, 43, 44, 47, 49, 51
Baez, Joan, 25
Bainbridge, Beryl, 19
Baker, Russell, 156

Baldridge, Letitia, 110
Balzac, Honoré de, 186, 189
Bankhead, Tallulah, 49
Banks, Tyra, 70
Bardot, Brigitte, 68
Barnes, Julian, 123
Barry, Dave, 84, 86, 98
Barrymore, John, 39, 119, 152, 197, 206
Basile, Matt, 193
Baudelaire, Charles-Pierre, 53, 194
Baum, Vicki, 183
Bean, Orson, 211
Beattie, Ann, 171
Beatty, Warren, 145
Beaumont, Lord, 74
Beauty, 28, 65–75, 93, 185. *See also* Appearance
Beauvoir, Simone de, 94, 196
Beck, Alan, 102
Beerbohm, Max, 43, 50
Behan, Brendan, 150, 200
Belmondo, Jean-Paul, 33
Bennett, Alan, 7, 44
Berger, John, 4
Bergman, Ingmar, 33
Bergman, Ingrid, 164
Bergson, Henri, 161
Bernard, Jeffrey, 129
Bernsen, Corbin, 90
Betti, Ugo, 141
Bible, The, 70, 174
Bierce, Ambrose, 13, 54, 102
Bigamy, 183, 188
Billings, Josh, 4, 17
Binger, William, 16
Biological clock, 73, 109
Bisexuals, 24
Bisset, Jacqueline, 175
Bitch (Wurtzel), 70
Bitches and witches, 39
Black, Karen, 138
Blackwell, Antoinette Brown, 26
Blackwell, Elizabeth, 164
Blake, Eubie, 140
Blakely, Mary Kay, 212
Blessington, Lady Marguerite Gardiner, 14, 68, 123
Blondes, 67
Bluestone, Ed, 143
Bly, Robert, 99

Body Heat (film), 86
Boerne, Ludwig, 49, 195
Bombeck, Erma, 173
Bonaparte, Napoleon, 42
Bondage, 112, 138
Boosler, Elayne, 37, 79
Bourget, Paul, 120
Bowen, Elizabeth, 35
Boyd, L. M., 160
Boys, 20, 22, 58, 101–4
Bradbury, Malcolm, 135
Brain, 43, 148, 150
Breasts, 34, 35, 36
Brecht, Bertolt, 13
Breton, André, 20
Brice, Fanny, 91, 97
Bride Walks Out, The (film), 177
Brides, 19. *See also* Weddings
Broderick, Helen, 177
Brookner, Anita, 44
Brooks, Mel, 122
Brophy, Brigid, 81, 163
Brothers, Joyce, 116, 187
Broun, Heywood C., 79, 162, 202
Brown, Helen Gurley, 129, 141
Brown, Joe E., 180
Brown, Rita Mae, 114, 205
Browning, Elizabeth Barrett, 103
Brush, Stephanie, 107
Bruyere, Jean de la, 121
Bryant, Anita, 140
Buddy Buddy (film), 209
Bukowski, Charles, 99
Bulwer-Lytton, Edward, 18
Bundy, Peg, 169
Burgess, Anthony, 150, 172
Burgess, Gelett, 29
Burnett, Carol, 28, 73
Burns, George, 134, 176, 198
Burroughs, John, 96
Burton, Robert, 158, 178
Buscaglia, Leo, 115
Butler, Samuel, 38
Buzzi, Ruth, 81
Byrd, Richard E., 41
Byrne, Robert, 78, 207
Byron, Lord, 174

Caan, James, 34
Caecilius, 196

Canady, Alexa, 57
Capote, Truman, 146
Carlin, George, 154
Carroll, Lewis, 104
Carson, Johnny, 211
Carter, Angela, 35, 71
Cartland, Barbara, 131
Casseres, Benjamin de, 45
Catcher in the Rye (Salinger), 155
Cats, 2
Caulfield, Holden, 155
Cervantes Saavedra, Miguel de, 55
Chamfort, Nicolas, 11, 51
Champagne, 40
Chandler, Raymond, 67
Chanel, Coco, 67, 72, 82
Chapelle, Dickey, 61
Chaperones, 52, 112
Chardin, Pierre Teilhard de, 26
Chase, Ilka, 97
Chastity, 56, 131, 165
Chazal, Malcolm de, 20
Chekhov, Anton, 71
Cher, 113
Chesterfield, Lord, 145
Chesterton, G. K., 94, 103
Chevalier, Maurice, 127
Childbearing, 25
Chisholm, Shirley, 62
Christina, Queen, 89
Churchill, Winston, 171, 175
Ciardi, John, 101
Cigars, 19, 42
Clairol ad slogan, 67
Clark, Blake, 88
Clayburgh, Jill, 34
Clergymen, 16
Cobb, Irvin S., 49
Cocktail parties, 116
Cole, William, 192
Coleridge, Samuel Taylor, 18, 171, 177
Colette, 58, 196
Collins, Jackie, 92
Colton, Charles Caleb, 126
Comfort, Alex, 93
Commitment, 82
Communication and conversation, 26, 84, 114
Compton-Burnett, Ivy, 2, 116
Computer dating, 115

Condoms, 137
Connery, Sean, 139
Connolly, Billy, 181
Connolly, Cyril, 5, 104, 168
Connolly, Marc, 156
Conrad, Joseph, 53
Conway, Tim, 203
Cooper, Gary, 99
Cope, Wendy, 61
Coquelin, Ernest, 193
Cosby, Bill, 25, 36
Cosmetics and makeup, 10, 64, 68, 69, 72
Coty perfume ad, 5
Courteline, Georges, 53
Coward, Noel, 172
Craik, Dinah Mulock, 115
Crashaw, Richard, 100
Crawford, Joan, 125
Crisp, Quentin, 145
Crying and tears, 19, 42, 88
Curtis, George William, 131

Dahlberg, Edward, 87
Dancing, 154
Dangerfield, Rodney, 188
Dating and relationships, 105–17
Davis, Bette, 40, 52, 79, 168, 202
Day, Doris, 29
Day, Lillian, 45
De Angelis, Barbara, 23, 98
Deadliness, 47
Death, 9, 11
Delaney, Shelagh, 46
DeLillo, Don, 57
Deneuve, Catherine, 210
Depardieu, Gerard, 139
Depew, Chauncey, 51
Derek, Bo, 66
DeVoto, Bernard, 42
Devries, Peter, 75, 178, 199
Diana, Princess, 210
Dickinson, Angie, 139
Dietrich, Marlene, 149, 150, 186
Dinesen, Isak, 16
Dior, Christian, 35
Directions, asking for, 79, 86
Disney, Walt, 125
Disraeli, Benjamin, 170, 175, 181
Distrust, 16, 39

Divorce, 130, 137, 201–12
Dix, Dorothea, 204
Dogs, 43, 81
Donne, John, 47
Douglas, Kirk, 169
Douglas, Michael, 78
Douglas, Norman, 193
Dowling, Colette, 116
Drinking, 38
Driving, 89
Dryden, John, 72, 192
Dumas, Alexandre, 20
Duncan, Isadora, 191
Dunne, Finley Peter, 100
Durning, Charles, 144
Durst, Will, 3, 136
Dutch treat, 64

Earhart, Amelia, 62
Education, 42
Ego, 78
Ehrenreich, Barbara, 63, 178
Ekland, Britt, 199
Eliot, George, 23, 25, 46
Eliot, T. S., 9
Ellerbee, Linda, 85
Ellis, Havelock, 141
Emerson, Ralph Waldo, 14, 95, 102
Encouragement, 22
Enemies, 91
Energy, 93
Englishmen, 162
Ephron, Nora, 40, 64, 76, 88, 151
Esar, Evan, 202
Euripides, 36, 200

Fabio, 112
Faithfull, Marianne, 114
Farewell, My Lovely (Chandler), 67
Fascination, 115
Fashion, 65–75
Fat Is a Feminist Issue (Orbach), 65
Fathers and fatherhood, 6, 100–101
Fathers-in-law, 188
Fear, 49, 50, 82, 98, 122
Feelings and emotions, 23, 37, 89
Feinstein, Dianne, 19
Feirstein, Bruce, 54
Femininity, 6, 57
Feminism, 56–65, 159

Fern, Fanny, 78
Ferris, Richard J., 6
Fetishism, 160
Fidelity, 197–200
Field, Sally, 142
Fielding, Henry, 181
Fields, W. C., 38, 40, 147
Fighting, 39
Finney, Eileen, 185
Fisher, Carrie, 35
Fitzgerald, F. Scott, 130
Flanner, Janet, 27
Fleming, Ian, 152, 181
Flight attendants and pilots, 6
Flirting, 39, 106, 107
Flowers, 113
Franklin, Benjamin, 11, 68, 180
Frederick, Pauline, 3
French, Marilyn, 85
Freud, Sigmund, 20, 32, 122
Friday, Nancy, 148
Friedan, Betty, 153
Friedman, Bruce, 106
Friendship, 17, 21, 40, 126
Frigidity, 91
Frost, Robert, 127
Fry, Stephen, 159
Fuller, Thomas, 189

Gable, Clark, 122
Gabor, Zsa Zsa, 89, 96, 207, 208, 209
Galbraithe, John Kenneth, 206
Galen, 146
Garfield, James A., 97
Gaskell, Elizabeth, 90
Gassman, Vittorio, 5
Gauguin, Paul, 157
Gay, John, 32, 121, 191
Gender gap, 1–29
Genuineness, 115
Geraldy, Paul, 130
Gide, André, 93
Gifts, 5, 14
Gilder, George, 155
Gilman, Charlotte Perkins, 15, 43
Gingold, Hermione, 149
Ginsberg, Allen, 158
Giovanni, Nikki, 151
Giraudoux, Jean, 90
Girls, 20, 22, 46, 58

Giroud, Francoise, 17
Glasses, 108
Glyn, Elinor, 131, 207
God, 1
Godwin, Gail, 12
Good women, 43, 44, 47, 49, 55
Goodman, Ellen, 114
Goodsell, Jane, 4
Gordon, Karen Elizabeth, 81
Gorer, Geoffrey, 190
Gourmont, Rémy de, 92
Grable, Betty, 27
Gracian, Baltasar, 69, 120
Grant, Cary, 206
Great men, 81
Greer, Germaine, 19, 87, 94, 149
Grizzard, Lewis, 146, 210
Groening, Matt, 2, 124
Guccionne, Bob, 145
Guilt, 50
Guitry, Sacha, 69, 190
Gynecologists, 14

Hamilton, William, 19
Happiness, 68
Harburg, E. Y., 124
Hardy, Thomas, 193
Harrison, Barbara Grizzuti, 18
Harrison, Jane, 27
Hawes, Elizabeth, 204
Hawn, Goldie, 199
Hazlitt, William, 174
Head, Edith, 67
Headaches, 136
Headroom, Max, 122
Heart, 15, 27, 48, 78, 129
Heilburn, Carolyn, 186
Heimel, Cynthia, 76
Heine, Heinrich, 42, 55, 197
Heinlein, Robert, 137
Heiresses, 72, 185
Heller, Joseph, 177
Hemingway, Ernest, 128, 169
Hempel, Amy, 112
Henry, O., 87, 95, 191
Hepburn, Katharine, 16, 59, 68, 75
Herbert, A. P., 181
Herold, Don, 41, 48, 157, 194
Heterosexuality, 151
Hiemel, Cynthia, 105

Hijazi, Muhammad, 17
Hilton, Conrad, 207
Historical romances, 131
Hoffman, Dustin, 5, 89, 144
Holly, Lauren, 73
Holm, Celeste, 80
Holmes, Oliver Wendell, Sr., 45
Homosexuals, 92, 140, 144, 158
Howard, Jane, 22
Howe, Edgar Watson, 11, 12, 19, 43,
    130, 188, 189, 193
Hubbard, Elbert, 15, 127, 173, 206
Hubbard, Kin, 101, 104, 195, 196
Hughes, Rupert, 112
Human Element in Sex, The (Blackwell),
    165
Humor, 10
Humphrey, Hubert, 184
Hurston, Zora Neale, 96
Husbands, 183–88
Hutton, Barbara, 185
Huxley, Aldous, 137, 165
Hysteria, 10

Imagination, 50
Indecent Exposure (film), 112
Inside Mr. Enderby (Burgess), 150
Insults, 187
Intellectuals, 137
Intelligence, 8, 23, 43, 44, 49, 58
Intimacy, 35
Intuition, 41, 112
Invention, 28
Irving, Washington, 91
Italian men, 92

Janeway, Elizabeth, 59
Jealousy, 125, 188
Jerry Maguire (film), 91
Jillson, Joyce, 106
Job interviews, 63
Joel, Billy, 138
Johnson, Lyndon B., 195
Johnson, Samuel, 58
Johnston, Jill, 47
Jones, Franklin P., 182
Jong, Erica, 8, 50, 183, 211
Joplin, Janis, 158
Joy of Sex, The (Comfort), 93
Juvenal, 55

Karr, Alphonse, 82
Kassenbaum, Nancy, 85
Katz, Jonathan, 198
Keillor, Garrison, 77, 83, 86, 142
Kempton, Sally, 20, 23
Kennedy, Florynce, 91
Kennedy, Rose Fitzgerald, 183
Kerr, Jean, 52, 84, 212
Keyes, Marian, 73
Kierkegaard, 53
King, Alan, 176
Kinison, Sam, 170
Kinsey, Alfred, 154, 164
Kinsey, Clara, 153
Kipling, Rudyard, 42, 47
Kissing, 18, 34, 48, 67, 90, 135, 164
Kissinger, Henry, 153
Klein, Calvin, 73
Kraus, Karl, 156, 159, 165
Kumin, Maxine, 13

La Rouchefoucauld, 55
Ladies, 45, 135
Lamarr, Hedy, 69
Landers, Ann, 13, 137, 138
Langdon-Davies, John, 174
Lansky, Bruce, 80, 135
Larkin, Phillip, 152
Lauder, Estee, 110
Laughter, 41, 149, 152, 183
Lawrence, D. H., 130
Lawyers, 80, 176, 212
Leacock, Stephen, 170
Learning, 26
Lebowitz, Fran, 31, 56, 113, 135, 151
Lee, Gypsy Rose, 142, 151
Legman, Gershon, 156
Lehrer, Tom, 46
Lemmon, Jack, 180
Lenclos, Ninon de, 25, 92, 94, 162
Lennon, John, 48
Lerner, Alan J., 32
Lerner, Harriet, 115, 117
Lesbians, 47
Lessing, Doris, 52
Levant, Oscar, 209
Levenson, Sam, 74
Levinger, George, 173
Lewis, Richard, 136
Life expectancy, 8

Life plan, 115
Lilly, Doris, 161
Limitations, 26, 95
Lincoln, Abraham, 107, 180
Lindbergh, Anne Morrow, 21
Little America, 41
Lockwood, Belva, 24
Lodge, David, 161
Loneliness, 168
Longfellow, Henry Wadsworth, 171
Lorde, Audre, 89
Loren, Sophia, 66, 67
Love and romance, 7, 14, 17, 20, 38, 53,
    81, 94, 96, 103, 119–31, 138,
    142, 144, 161, 172
Lowell, Amy, 125
Lubbock, John, 20
Lynes, Russell, 45
Lynn, Loretta, 74

Macho, 84, 89
MacKenzie, Compton, 38
MacLaine, Shirley, 150
Madonna, 138
Maher, Bill, 144
Mailer, Norman, 143, 158, 203, 209
Malkovich, John, 71
Manliness, 27
Mannes, Marya, 22, 46
Mansfield, Jayne, 90
Mansfield, Katherine, 120
Manville, Tommy, 203
Marbury, Elizabeth, 59
Markoe, Merrill, 107
Marriage, 9, 12, 14, 26, 36, 62, 88, 91,
    94, 168–83
"Married with Children" (television
    program), 169
Martin, Dick, 173
Martin, Steve, 139
Marvin, Lee, 33
Marx, Groucho, 65, 90, 147, 184, 198,
    206, 208
Marx, Karl, 64
Masculinity, 6
Mason, Jackie, 198
Masturbation, 140, 147
Maugham, W. Somerset, 126, 184
McCabe, Charles, 198
McCullough, Colleen, 37

McDonald, Walter, 202
McDowell, Mary, 3
McGinley, Phyllis, 10, 22, 75
McInerney, Jay, 114
McLaughlin, Mignon, 124, 172
Meir, Golda, 7
Men, 78–98
Mencken, H. L., 8, 9, 15, 18, 19, 39, 56,
    175, 177, 184, 188, 199
Metalious, Grace, 160
Michelangelo, 194
Mickey Mouse, 125
Mid-life crisis, 185
Midler, Bette, 147
Miller, Alice Duer, 98
Miller, Arthur, 130
Miller, Dennis, 195
Miller, Henry, 148, 155
Miller, Larry, 81
Millett, Kate, 52
Milton, John, 54
Mirman, Sophie, 37
Misfits, 46
Misogyny, 56
Mistinguett, 34
Mizner, Wilson, 50
Modesty, 24, 25
Money and wealth, 16, 22, 26, 27, 38,
    55, 110, 185, 196
Monogamy, 10, 86, 145, 183, 188, 199
Monroe, Marilyn, 79, 95, 160
Monroe, Vaughn, 205
Montand, Yves, 199
Morgan, Marabel, 38
Morley, Christopher, 82
Mortimer, John, 10
Moss, Stirling, 89
Mothers and motherhood, 6, 7, 8, 12,
    73–76
Mothers-in-law, 184, 193
Movies, 33, 157
Ms., 35
Muggeridge, Malcolm, 150, 153
Muir, Charles, 147
Murdoch, Iris, 129
Murphy, Maureen, 84
Music, 138, 141

Nachman, Gerald, 175
Namath, Joe, 155

Nash, Ogden, 44, 69
Nathan, George Jean, 10, 41, 45, 114,
    145, 157, 163
Nation, Carry, 95
Nature, 26, 58
Navratilova, Martina, 24
Neckties, 85
Neuroses, 130
Nicholson, Harold, 179
Nietzsche, Friedrich, 61, 91
Nimitz, Chester, 65
Norris, Kathleen, 205
Northwest Mounted Police (film), 99
Nudity, 66, 70, 71
Nuns, 138

Oakley, Ann, 33
Oates, Joyce Carol, 126
O'Brien, Edna, 65
Obscenity, 48
O'Connor, Frank, 57
O'Connor, Joey, 8
Odets, Clifford, 152
Older women, 19, 37, 152
One-night stands, 139
Ono, Yoko, 60
Opportunity, 55
Optimism, 51
Orbach, Susie, 65
Orgasm, 54, 152
O'Rourke, P. J., 39, 135, 190
Ovid, 42, 56, 86, 128, 134

Paglia, Camille, 63, 85, 159
Parker, Dorothy, 9, 108, 148
Parton, Dolly, 66, 206
Partridge, Alan, 134
Patinkin, Mark, 109
Patterson, Isabel, 15
Payne, Cynthia, 159
Peckinpah, Sam, 153
Penney, Alexandra, 108
People's Republic of China, 144
Perfume, 67, 84
Perkins, Frances, 62
Perrine, Valerie, 154
Pessimism, 51
Philip, Prince, 189
Picasso, Pablo, 48
Pierce, Charles, 110

Piercy, Marge, 46, 159, 160
Pierson, Elaine, 149
Piper, Monica, 112
Pizzey, Erin, 3
Plato, 101
PMS, 88
Pogrebin, Letty Cottin, 108, 161
Politics, 62, 85
Pope, 145
Porter, Eleanor H., 22
Porter, Katherine Anne, 79
Poverty, 38
Power, 2, 23, 58, 153
Prayer, 141
Priest, Ivy Baker, 27
Promiscuity, 137
Propertius, 51
Prostitutes, 41, 52, 200
Proverbs, 75, 122, 179
   African, 200
   American, 197
   Chinese, 28
   Estonian, 190
   French, 201
   German, 72, 100, 200
   Greek, 180
   Hebrew, 74
   Italian, 72
   Japanese, 190
   Mexican, 183
   Russian, 191
   Scottish, 70
   Spanish, 50
   Yiddish, 210
Prudes, 52
Pryce-Jones, David, 182
Pryor, Richard, 176
Psychoanalysis, 20

Qualifying, 13
Quant, Mary, 73
Quinn, Anthony, 78

Race, 62
Ramey, Estelle, 8
Rand, Ayn, 137
Rankin, Jeannette, 17
Rape, 85
Reagan, Nancy, 47
Récamier, Mme., 43

Recipes, 18
Reik, Theodor, 2, 9, 144
Reincarnation, 148
Remarriage, 202, 203, 205, 207, 209, 210
Remembering, 3, 9
Rescue fantasies, 105
Respect, 28
Reynolds, Burt, 138
Rivarol, Antoine de, 40
Rivers, Joan, 143, 204
Robertson, Nan, 5
Rock, Chris, 88
Rogers, Will, 71, 200
Rohatyn, Felix, 160
Ronstadt, Linda, 138
Rooney, Mickey, 152, 211
Roseanne, 63
Rosenberg, Helena Hacker, 36
Rosenberg, Joel, 82
Rostand, Jean, 194
Rotten, Johnny, 128
Rousseau, Jean-Jacques, 15
Rovin, Jeff, 135
Rowland, Helen, 7, 54, 83, 107, 128, 168
Rubin, Bob, 136
Rubinstein, Artur, 164
Rubinstein, Helena, 24, 68
Rudner, Rita, 108, 109, 167, 187
Russell, Bertrand, 101, 126

Sagan, Françoise, 66
Sahl, Mort, 81
Sailing, 116
St. James, Susan, 109
St. Johns, Adela Rogers, 184
Saint-Exupéry, Antoine de, 120
Saki, 71
Salinger, J. D., 155
Santayana, George, 21
Sarandon, Susan, 34
Sather, Drake, 192
Savalas, Telly, 136
Savannah, Susan, 84
Scarlet Letter, The (Hawthorne), 198
Schickel, Richard, 82
Schlafly, Phyllis, 61
Scholars and scholarship, 61, 135
Schwarzenegger, Arnold, 33

Scott-Maxwell, Florida, 76
Seduction, 151
Segal, Erich, 122, 129
Seger, Bob, 108
Sellars, Peter, 34
Sex, 2, 14, 36, 60, 90, 92, 107, 133–65
Sex appeal, 162
Sex change, 21
Sex Is Never an Emergency (Pierson), 149
Sex symbols, 160
Sexual equality, 5, 10, 11, 17, 24, 27, 39, 58, 81
Sexual fantasies, 151, 152
Sexual response, 93
Shakespeare, William, 37, 130, 182
Shandling, Garry, 110
Sharman, Helen, 2
Shaw, George Bernard, 12, 80, 120, 144
Sheehy, Gail, 7
Sheen, Archbishop Fulton J., 153
Shelley, Mary Wollstonecraft, 6
Shepard, Sam, 121
Sheridan, Richard Brinsley, 76, 140
Shields, Brooke, 139
Shopping, 42
Shore, Dinah, 24
Shriner, Will, 143
Siegel, Max, 176
Simon, Neil, 72
Singles, 25, 37
Siskind, Carol, 142
Skelton, Red, 186
Skelton, Tressa, 211
Sleeper (film), 148
Small talk, 93
Smiley, Jane, 115, 179
Smith, Adam, 93
Smith, Logan Pearsall, 62
Smith, Marion, 81
Smith, Sydney, 16
Snoring, 172
Snow, Carrie, 14, 176
Socks, 44
Socrates, 191
Some Like It Hot (film), 180
Sontag, Susan, 6
Space travel, 2
Spacks, Patricia Meyer, 4, 28
Spark, Muriel, 113, 158
Spingarn, Joel E., 16

Staël, Madame de, 98
Stanwyck, Barbara, 177
Star Wars (film), 35
Stark, Dame Freya, 44
Steinem, Gloria, 26, 56, 58, 60, 64, 88, 177
Stendhal, 37, 126, 128
Stevenson, Adlai, 101
Stewart, James, 68
Stomach, 78
Streisand, Barbra, 187
Strength, 23, 47
Stubborness, 90
Success, 80, 98, 117, 168, 203
Sunshine, Linda, 112
Swanson, Gloria, 208
Szasz, Thomas, 2, 140

Talleyrand, 55
Talmud, 38
Tannen, Deborah, 93
Tarkington, Booth, 102
Tax, Meredith, 205
Temptation, 19, 157
Tenuta, Judy, 113
Thackeray, William, 53
Thales, 179
Theories about the sexes, 28
Thomas, Marlo, 14, 60
Thoreau, Henry David, 97
Thurber, James, 12, 104, 127, 187
Tilsner, Julie, 106
Toilet seats, 8
Tomlin, Lily, 72, 129
Tongue, 54
Tootsie (film), 144
Toscanini, Arturo, 48
Total women, 38
Toughness, 19
Toynbee, Polly, 74
Treveleyan, John, 154
Trevino, Lee, 195, 205
Trevor, Claire, 204
Trust, 60
Turner, Kathleen, 86, 92
Turner, Lana, 168
Twain, Mark, 103, 121, 146
Tweedie, Jill, 59
29 and Counting: A Chick's Guide to Turning 30 (Tilsner), 106

Ulrich, Laurel Thatcher, 65
Underground issues, 117
Updike, John, 144
Ustinov, Peter, 147

Valéry, Paul, 49, 125
Van Buren, Abigail, 75, 109, 194
Van Doren, Mamie, 180
Vanbrugh, John, 48
Vanderbilt, Amy, 52
Vanity, 4, 24
Vasectomy, 143
Vass, Susan, 170
Vaughan, Bill, 54
Vicious, Sid, 123
Viorst, Judith, 123, 127
Virginia Slims ad slogan, 59
Virgins, 87
Virtue, 24, 55
Voltaire, 207
Vonnegut, Kurt, 42
Vos Savant, Marilyn, 28
Voting, 65, 97

War correspondent, 61
War of the sexes, 5, 11, 128
Warhol, Andy, 124, 141, 145
Waters, John, 133
Waugh, Evelyn, 21, 152
Wayne, John, 58
Weddings, 196–97
Weight, 22
Weisstein, Naomi, 23
Welch, Raquel, 162
Weld, Tuesday, 156
Welles, Orson, 60, 83
Wells, H. G., 163
West, Mae, 50, 86, 90, 94, 164, 182
West, Rebecca, 13, 57, 88

Westheimer, Ruth, 162
White, E. B., 127, 187
Whitehorn, Katherine, 58, 87, 157
Whitley, 74
Whitton, Charlotte, 64
Whores, 70, 87, 153
Widows, 190, 191
Wiest, Dianne, 168
Wilde, Oscar, 7, 32, 39, 47, 188, 197,
    212
Wilder, Thornton, 51, 189
Williams, Tennessee, 10, 39
Williamson, Nicol, 41
Wilson, August, 95, 96
Wilson, Earl, 157
Winters, Shelley, 67, 170
Wisdom, 9, 28
Wives, 188–96
Wodehouse, P. G., 203
Womanliness, 27
Women, 32–56
*Women Are Always Right and Men Are
    Never Wrong* (O'Connor), 8
Women's roles, 56–65
Women's studies, 63
Wood, Natalie, 9
Wood, Victoria, 21
Woodward, Joanne, 183
Woolfe, Virginia, 36
Work and careers, 58, 59, 63, 88,
    169
Writing, 36, 40, 94
Wurtzel, Elizabeth, 70

Younger men, 19, 37
Youngman, Henny, 123, 169

Zander, Robin, 145
Zellweger, Renee, 91